RECLAIMING WESTERN CULTURES

SIMON LENNON

Reclaiming Western Cultures
Non-fiction
Cultural Policy, Christianity
A book in the collection: The West
A book in the series: Cultures
Published by Pine Hill Books
Copyright © 2016, 2020 by Simon Lennon.
All rights reserved.
This book or any portion thereof may not be reproduced, stored in or introduced into a retrieval system, or transmitted in any form or by any means whatsoever (electronic, mechanical, photocopying, recording, or otherwise) without the express written prior permission of the author and the publisher, except for the use of brief quotations in a book review, scholarly journal, or student assignment.
The author asserts his moral rights.
ISBN 978-1-925446-03-6 (electronic)
ISBN 978-1-925446-19-7 (paperback)
52,000 words, plus bibliography, references to 56,000 words
Cover image: Iandra, 2012

In memory of my paternal grandmother's mother

CONTENTS

1. Diasporas 1
2. Christmas Day, 1914 8
3. Eternity 16
4. Religion by Race 22
5. Enlightenment 29
6. Vanishing Us 37
7. Multiculturalism 45
8. The Religion of Europe 53
9. Perspectives 60
10. Cultureless Individualism 68
11. Owning Culture 75
12. Who We Are 83
13. Art 89
14. Architecture and Design 97
15. Homes and Houses 103
16. Music 107
17. Prose and Poetry 113
18. Films 120
19. Television 127
20. Cultural Revisionism 135
21. Haute Couture 145
Bibliography, References 153
About the Author 168

1. DIASPORAS

I am not an individual, at least not just an individual. The more millions and billions of people there are in the world, the more solitary each individual becomes.

"All the great nations of the earth have what the Jews call a diaspora," Quintin McGarel Hogg told Britain's House of Commons in 1968. "The Jews have it, the British have it, the Irish have a diaspora, the Chinese have an enormous diaspora, so have the Arabs, the Indians, and the Pakistanis."

A diaspora means more than people dispersing from their homeland. It's a continuing sense of collective identity: a cogent whole encompassing them, their generations passed, and their generations to come. It links them all to their ancient land wherever they are, no less their ancestral home if they've never been there. However long ago their ancestors departed and however many countries they've traversed, they enjoy and suffer their diaspora.

In 1950, black American Malcolm Little rejected his surname for being a slave name. Unable to know his family name, he chose to be called Malcolm X. His father had been a Baptist minister, but still he came to consider Christianity the white people's religion. (Only white people imagine religion to be separate from culture and them both to be separate from race, unless we're rebuking each other for appropriating other races' cultures.) Malcolm X became a Muslim, changing his name again to El-Hajj Malik El-Shabazz.

Despite having an English grandfather and other traces of European blood, by 1964 he rejected racial integration. Blaming high crime rates among black Americans upon the decadent mores of white society, he believed black people should govern themselves. He urged them to return home to Africa. Many did, before he decided Africans had no need to return. They could recover their peace of mind and self-respect by identifying with Africa: by being African Americans. He sought to unify the African diaspora.

Descendants of African slaves brought to the Americas have only their continental diaspora. Recent African immigrants know their tribal origins. They're Africans and more.

New York Giants footballer Mathias Kiwanuka was born in Indianapolis and called it his hometown, but his homeland was that of his ancestors. "How much does Uganda mean to me?" he asked in 2012, the week before his team played in the Super Bowl. "It means everything."

Increasing emigration led Indians across the Asia–Pacific to come together annually by race. In 2013, New South Wales welcomed a thousand of them to Sydney for their seventh gathering. "The aim of the Regional Pravasi Bharatiya Divas, or Overseas Indian Conference, is to connect India with its vast Indian diaspora and bringing their knowledge, expertise, and skills together," said Premier Barry O'Farrell. "New South Wales is honoured to be a part of this fantastic event."

Diasporas mean most when a people are attacked, or even just mocked. When American actor Alec Baldwin joked about "getting a Filipina mail-order bride" in 2009, I suspect most of the furore came from white Americans. One press report referred to him angering the huge Filipino diaspora.

Speaking of the Jewish diaspora has fallen from favour, but diaspora it is: the original Diaspora. "I find as I get older," said actor Warren Mitchell, born Warren Misell, in 2008, "I'm feeling more and more Jewish." Born in Britain, he was an Australian citizen. "Maybe it's time I visited Israel."

I imagine many of us finding our diaspora more important as we age. I am. I didn't always think as I think now.

I'm not sure anyone alive knows how many generations ago my forebears left Ireland, Scotland, and England: eight perhaps, seven, or nine. It was sometime in the nineteenth, or possibly late eighteenth, century. My mother, long passed away, would have known. There were never many Brackpools in the world and they came from England; my mother's paternal something-cousins lived in Surrey. If our Mother Country wasn't the United Kingdom, she was Mother Ireland: the Emerald Isle. If none of my forebears came from Wales, then certainly some of my wife's forebears did. Our children's family is my family too.

From Europe, we children of empires came. We explored the world with Europe at our back, when Europe's children shone with our diasporas, but diasporas are racial. We've felt less and less of them since two world wars we so painfully won and more painfully lost.

We no longer explore. Europe is no longer at our back.

The West lost our sense of diaspora. We've become individuals, without consideration or comprehension of being more than we already are, without thinking about it. Unwilling to link ourselves with our ancestors or anyone else in particular, we care little what our forebears reasoned. We associate ourselves with our ancestral homelands no more than with Timbuktu.

We might even associate ourselves more with Timbuktu. We think the Malians need us.

In our postmodern, multicultural West, the adjectives by which we call people African Americans and so forth aren't supposed to be racial descriptors, since we no longer believe in race. They're geographical, ancestral pasts, but we descendants of those who left Europe don't call ourselves European. French Canadians aren't Canadian French, but French-speaking Canadians. It's a matter of language, not ancestry. Our ancestors don't matter.

Nor do we call those of us living in Africa or Asia, Africans or Asians. We're whites, as blacks and browns sometimes still are but reds and yellows never still are. We're Caucasians, as Negroes and Mongoloids no longer are, but not from any last reverence for science in our treatment of race. Nor are we claiming ancestral links to the Caucasus between Europe and Asia. We're just grappling for a word akin to race other than being European. We're people without ancestry.

Europe becomes just a place. We treat being European as living there. Non-Europeans aren't. We want to ensure immigrants there feel no less European for having forebears from somewhere else.

If descendants of ancient European peoples allowed in ourselves what we respect in others, we'd again feel our diasporas. We'd be what we are, wherever we are. Europe's sometimes wayward children dispersed through the rest of the world would again be European. Other races would not, not even in Europe. We'd look upon our ancestral homelands as other races look upon theirs. We'd rediscover Europe and her colonies. Were we to take other races' lead, we'd reunify our diasporas.

We'd be not just Australians but British too, however many generations ago we left our Isles. My children would savour

Mother Ireland, Britain, and Europe, without begrudging other races their mothers too. Americans might be Germans too. For those of us carrying the blood of more than one European people, New Zealanders could be Scandinavians too, Alabamans Europeans too.

A British diaspora was the reason his father sent my father (with his mother) to London to complete his education in 1953. There he saw Princess Elizabeth became Her Majesty Queen Elizabeth II. We colonial sons and daughters weren't foreigners in Britain then, in anybody's eyes.

Britain was too far away for my childhood family's only overseas holiday to be there, in 1977. My mother's Francophilia might've been the reason we visited French colonial New Caledonia.

In November 1979, while summer rose in Australia, my father took seventeen-year-old me to late-autumn Europe. The trip was my reward for completing the last two years of high school and so something like the completion of my education (except that I was headed to university as no one in my family had previously been). Great cathedrals, palaces, and squares had been storybooks and folklore to boys and girls raised on the far side of the world. What had been pictures and moving images in film and television became cool streets on which we walked and cold stones I tentatively touched. In the company of old London, Mother England and I made each other real. We weren't strangers as much as we might have imagined.

Six and a half years later, finished with my undergraduate studies, I returned with my girlfriend to London, continuing my education. Moving onto more Europe, an Irish diaspora might have been the reason the first country we visited after the United Kingdom was Ireland.

A plaque in Galway commemorated the speech America's President John Kennedy delivered there twenty-three years earlier, near the end of his first visit to the land of his forebears. "It is strange," said Kennedy, the penultimate day of June 1963, "that so many years could pass and so many generations pass and still some of us who came on this trip could come home and, here to Ireland, and feel ourselves at home and not feel ourselves in a strange country, but feel ourselves among neighbours, even though we are separated by generations, by time, and by thousands of miles."

I felt the same. I'd come home.

Twelve years after my first visit there, on Saint Paddy's Day 1998, I again stood in Galway. With me were my wife and our infant son and daughter. We'd all come home.

The West doesn't cease being European, because we think we've ceased. When I describe people as being Western or European, I refer to we whose ancestors came from Europe. Where we were born doesn't matter. Nor does it matter, for these purposes, whether we live in Europe or elsewhere. We're no less European for being colonial European.

When Western peoples feel our diasporas early in the twenty-first century, we do so with contempt. Journalist David Penberthy called Britain's Diamond Jubilee celebrations *"cringeworthy"* in an article published the Queen's Birthday weekend Sunday, 2012. For those few days commemorating sixty years since the coronation of Queen Elizabeth II, Britons (nostalgically, perhaps) had celebrated being British.

"The images we saw this week of Britain in 2012 looked remarkably like Australia in the 1960s and 1970s," Penberthy disdained of his heritage. He scorned his people wanting to keep our culture, as if our culture were worth keeping.

I would never ask other races to celebrate our cultures, but it would be nice if we celebrated them. They're all that we have.

"These days," wrote Penberthy, *"younger Australians with an urge to get away and get ahead are increasingly likely to look to Asia or the Americas than the once-glorious motherland."* Young people don't know what they're missing, because we tell them they're not missing anything; people are confined by whatever they know. When those who were there speak of the past, we don't hear their elderly memories.

"Most Australians have embraced or at least tolerate the concept of multiculturalism." (We'd resigned to what our rulers command.) *"Generally speaking we are proud of and recognise the contribution which successive waves of migration have made to Australia. The concerns which Pauline Hanson voiced just sixteen years ago in her maiden speech – "I believe we are being swamped by Asians" – seem kind of hilarious given that through the good fortune of our geography we have an Asian enterprise culture at home, and massive export markets and a rapidly-growing middle class right on our doorstep."*

Just because the West stopped believing anything worthwhile doesn't mean everyone else has. While we criticise what smidgeons remain of Western cultures, we admire other races retaining theirs. Outside the West, most countries enjoy cultural and racial homogeneity, content to be left in their peace. We don't call them backward, bland, or insular as we describe our past homogeneity. We don't criticise their monocultures, traditions, and values. What Penberthy called Asian enterprise culture meant their obsession with business, replacing what had been our culture. We holiday in their countries of origin.

All Australians celebrate is other races. We think we'd be failures without them.

"*As Britain continues to define itself desperately and defiantly through its Anglo monoculture, Australia has spent the past three decades becoming prouder of its diversity and more comfortable with its place in the world.*" (Our population no longer cared that Australia doesn't exist, which Penberthy thought was terrific. We serve the countries that do.) "*We are located in the engine room of the world economy, with China and India to the north, Brazil and Chile to the east.*" (Our economies build empires, but not ours.) "*And Great Britain is stuck in once-great Europe, where bloated, incompetent, profligate governments threaten the world economic order.*"

Penberthy went onto quote Englishman Theodore Dalrymple writing in *The Spectator* magazine. "*At the start of the reign whose 60th anniversary we 'celebrate', Britain was one of the best-ordered societies in western Europe,*" wrote Dalrymple. "*Now, sixty years later, it is easily the most crime-ridden. Unpleasant social disorder is everywhere…our police, once a model to the world, increasingly resemble an occupying army. The state of the country is parlous in more ways than one. Large areas, once industrial, resemble the Soviet Union with takeaway pizza. The only 'private' enterprise consists of retail chains…the middle class in such areas is composed almost entirely of public employees and professionals who cater to the social problems caused by mass unemployment.*"

Our English culture we've come to despise worked well, one of the best ordered societies of 1952 that Dalrymple described. We don't imagine Britain's problems nowadays being due to multiculturalism, but to trying to save something of being British. The essence of Australia's multiculturalism, like that of New Zealand, America, and Canada, is that we're discarding our countries and cultures. Abandoning ourselves to our immigrants, we have little left to retain, little to get in the way. We struggle whenever we try.

If the West believes all races and cultures are equal, then we'll do what other races do. We'll reclaim our cultures.

That Sunday I read Penberthy's article, I sat among the congregation in our parish Anglican church: a high church myriad of Protestantism and Catholicism calling itself Anglo-Catholic, with a preacher called a father and Stations of the Cross. Hidden behind brick and stone walls, amidst our art and architecture, ours is the Church of England. There's a wealth of our cultural inheritance we rarely notice around us. If we do notice, we don't consider it ours.

Choral evensong each month is a complete cultural experience, with ritual and incense. Traditions express our connectedness with our forebears and theirs with us, supplementing biology with feeling. Cultures do the same for races. We stood that Sunday to sing in unison 'God Save the Queen', 'Jerusalem,' and 'I vow to thee, my country.'

Our congregation is often no more than a few dozen worshipers. Most are much older than I am, and proud.

If we care about generations after ours, we'll explore generations before ours, before politics and purchasing mattered so much. We'll rediscover what we did before all we did was work, shop, and dine in other people's restaurants. We'll sense something greater than our momentary commercial interests: a greater well-being than anything economic. Among the treasures our forebears can bring us, we'll find again fine arts.

We might feel as our forebears felt, becoming what we can be: peoples enjoying being ourselves, with everything full lives can offer. If we're to be more than politics and economics permit us to be, then we need to be more to begin with.

With heritages, we'll have futures. We need to learn of our peoples to learn who we are. If we can't be ourselves then nobody can, and we can't meaningfully be anyone else.

2. CHRISTMAS DAY, 1914

My paternal grandmother's mother grew up with gaslights brightening the streets of Sydney, before electricity arrived. She died close to ninety-one years of age in 1969, having seen a human being first walk upon the moon. No other generation had seen such change, although I've only the faintest recollections of her as an old woman struggling to move around. Technology is no substitute for civilisation, and my father said she often lamented through her long life, "Civilisation died in France in the Great War."

The ages of history rarely begin or end upon nicely defined dates at neatly defined places. My French friend Patrick placed the end of civilisation in Belgium in 1914. Germany, hitherto the most honourable of peoples, thought she could end the war quickly by frightening local villagers. She failed. If civilisation that previously seemed inviolable didn't die in 1914, it certainly began to fray.

The time remained one of honour. Captain Robert Campbell, aged twenty-nine, from Kent fought in northern France. In August 1914, Germans captured him and sent him to a prisoner-of-war camp in Germany.

Two years later, Campbell learnt that his mother Louisa back home in Kent was dying of cancer. He wrote to Kaiser Wilhelm II pleading to be allowed to visit her. The Kaiser permitted him to do so, provided he gave his word that he would return to Germany.

Campbell spent a week with his mother before she died in February 1917. He then returned to Germany, remaining a prisoner until the end of the war.

When my great-grandparents were born, the familial links between monarchs should have avoided wars in Europe, but in 1914 we stared each other down. Estimates vary, but fifteen or more million people died and more than twenty million people were wounded through that incomprehensible four-year war and the malnutrition and disease it wreaked, with more casualties in the Russian Civil War and Turkish War of Independence it bequeathed. When a man I met almost a century later spoke of the Great War wasting all the wealth Europeans had amassed since the Industrial Revolution, I told him we'd lost more than that. In the killing fields of France, we lost our self-belief.

European peoples, whether in the Americas, Europe, Australasia, or elsewhere, didn't all lose our self-belief at once. We punished a defeated Germany as if the Great War had been her fault alone, although she was no more responsible than other combatants. Nevertheless, she rose from her rut and rot. She rebuilt her self-belief and became again impressive, until France, Britain, and their empires declared more war upon her. The peace previously supposed to be eternal wasn't. The Great War became known as World War I, the First horrible World War, when World War II made world war repetitious.

The Second horrible World War scared us from ourselves: from ever wanting self-belief again. Europe's colonies and war-weary Europe herself came not to feel European, for fear we'd think too well of ourselves. We came to dread where race and nation took us. Two world wars and a holocaust condemned us to a coincidence of disillusion, from which we've still not recovered.

Without the Great War, there'd have been no Soviet communism, Nazism, or Holocaust. There'd be no multiculturalism.

Culture was intrinsic to the civilisation our empires spread around the world. When we lost confidence in our civilisation, we lost confidence in our culture. If they'd not brought us to war, they'd not saved us from it either. We ceased valuing our heritage and history, feeling we can't collectively do anything worthwhile.

Attending church weekly had been normal before the Great War, especially among the well-to-do. After the Great War, it ceased being normal. After World War II, it became unusual.

We lost confidence in Christianity not in spite of it being our religion, but because it was our religion. Science had nothing to do with it. Neither did God. Caught up with war, God ceased being a question of fact. This was no carefully reasoned analysis, but a failure of faith. Everything about us fell from repute.

It wasn't meant to be this way. "*Erected in Memory and Honour of those who went out from St Ives to fight in defence of COUNTRY, FREEDOM and CIVILIZATION*," says the plaque on a typical Great War memorial. The capitalisation was meant to be striking.

"*Unveiled 1922.*" Theirs was among the last generations for which civilisation was plainly European. Freedom was intrinsic to having a country, so the freedom was ours, along with a conviction we brought freedom and civilisation to other races. "*They sacrificed themselves to preserve their Country's heritage.*"

We can't understand the world since the Second World War without understanding that war in all its facets, but we can't understand that war without understanding the First and its aftermath. Hell, I don't understand, but I know the boys who fought and died rallied for God and Country. We did all our best deeds for God and Country, even if the people leading us to war did not.

We confuse causes of war with reasons our men volunteered to serve: the trusts, confidences, and loyalties. Remembering our memorials with talk of God and Country, we don't want them leading us to die. We gave them up not in spite of our forebears dying for us, but because so many of them did. Trying to take away reasons for war, refusing for us their reasons to fight, we gave up what we valued rather than risk coalescing around them. Slowly, we're discarding the remnants of civilisation for which we fought, killed, and died.

A century later, when white people without faith think about religion (beyond our platitudes for other religions), they're not very kind. They repeat our mantra without challenge, "Look at all the wars religion causes."

Not just separating themselves from Christianity, they're freeing Islam and other religions from specific blame for warmongering and terrorism. They reject religion not for any argument about the existence of God but because different religions separate people from each other, from which they think all war arises.

Atheist and agnostic killing, they're not even contemplating. From the French Revolution beginning in 1789, Western talk of political left and right arose. Rejecting Christianity, demanding liberty and equality, the Reign of Terror executed more than forty thousand Frenchmen, including clergymen and women.

"What wars does religion cause?" I ask, whenever anyone repeats the mantra to me.

World War I wasn't a conflict between religions. The Muslim Ottoman Empire fought alongside Protestant Germany and Roman Catholic Austro-Hungary. They fought against Orthodox

Russia, Roman Catholic France, and Protestant Britain. Jews were in most if not all the Christian armies.

Religion didn't cause World War II. Japan and its emperor were no more Christian than a bowl of sushi. I'm unaware of any historian proposing that Shintoism, Buddhism, or any other religion motivated Japanese aggression. If Christianity was involved in the Asian war, it was Christian Americans and other European peoples defeating Japan in 1945. So did the atheist Soviet Union.

A Great War veteran, a decorated war hero no less, Austrian-born Adolf Hitler became German chancellor in 1933 and dictator in 1934. Germany was Protestant, but Hitler had been raised a Roman Catholic, becoming an altar boy. Nothing in Catholicism explained Hitler's willingness to invade Roman Catholic Czechoslovakia, Poland, or France, while he made great efforts to avoid war with Protestant Britain. Roman Catholic Spain and Portugal kept out of the war altogether.

Underpinning any claim that religion caused World War II is the allegation it caused the Jewish Holocaust, the *Shoah*. In his 1925 manifesto *Mein Kampf*, Hitler cited the Lord God to justify anti-Semitism, but he ceased being part of any church long before gaining political office. He may well have stopped identifying with Christianity at all, while exploiting other people's faiths.

By the time of the Holocaust, Hitler made several comments highly critical of Christianity. "The heaviest blow that ever struck humanity was the coming of Christianity," he told Martin Bormann and other close associates, among a series of informal, private conversations often late at night or in early morning between July 1941 and June 1942, which Bormann recorded *ex tempore*. "Bolshevism is Christianity's illegitimate child. Both are inventions of the Jew."

No Christian called Christianity an invention of Jews, not then. He might've been right about Bolshevism (as communism was then known), but we're not about to believe anything Hitler thought.

Hitler had almost certainly long been an atheist, but remains a clear example of a European we identify as being Christian quite apart from his views of God. So might he, if he wasn't simply manipulating General Gerhard Engel by telling him in 1941, "I am now as before a Catholic and will always remain so."

Christianity was the religion of Europe, the religion of Germans and Austrians, and so the religion of Hitler. He was born a Christian and so remained a Christian, however much he rejected Christianity and however much he might've feared being a quarter Jewish.

The perpetrators of war mightn't have been Christian. The victims often were. My house tutor for three years and fourth-form English teacher John Groenewegen was the son of a Dutch clergyman imprisoned by the Nazis during World War II, as I learnt at his funeral thirty-six years after I finished school. A group of Polish nuns was among the prisoners upon whom physician Josef Mengele performed medical experiments at the Birkenau concentration camp, Auschwitz. As many as two thousand Roman Catholic clergy died in the Holocaust. They're not the victims we recall.

The men who left their homes and families from July 1914 went to fight the war to end all wars, they thought, so their countries would never again need fight, thinking they'd be home by Christmas. The trenches of the Western Front were rarely far apart. That Christmas Eve, the bitter cold froze the slush to ice. Soldiers normally remained in darkness, unwilling to light a cigarette for fear the speck of burning ash would betray their position and draw a sniper's shot, but in so cold and long a night as Christmas Eve, young German soldiers started lighting candles. The lights atop poles and bayonets illuminated their positions.

Young British soldiers didn't shoot. Peering through their binoculars, they saw Germans holding Christmas trees above their heads with candles burning in the branches. Without other means of communicating to their enemies across the night, the Germans (who every day for months on end had been trying to kill them and whom they'd been trying to kill) were wishing them a brave and humble Merry Christmas.

A few Germans began singing carols. Soon, Germans all along the lines were singing with them. "*Stille Nacht*," sung forth their melody, "*Heilige Nacht*."

The British recognised the harmony. "Silent night," they sung in unison, "Holy night."

Across the tortured night on wretched ground, where a generation across Europe and her empires was bleeding to the death, the Holy Mother's love and Child made something beautiful. They were no longer soldiers killing each other and themselves, but compatriots in Christendom. "*We stuck up a board with Merry Christmas on it,*" wrote Frank Richards in his diary. "*The enemy stuck up a similar one.*"

At several places along the battlefront, other Germans and British did the same. "People would shout messages like: 'Fritz, here. I was a waiter in a Manchester hotel before the war. How are my friends from the Lancashire?'" reported Peter Simkins of London's Imperial War Museum in 1996. "And, this went on in some parts for two or three days."

Soldiers along both lines laid down their weapons on Christmas Day, peering tentatively above the trenches. Without gunfire trying to kill them, they ventured cautiously up the steep trench walls to no man's land, where a day earlier was only death. "*Two of our men threw their equipment off and jumped on the parapet with their hands above their heads as two of the Germans did the same,*" wrote Richards, "*our two going to meet them. They shook hands and then we all got out of the trench and so did the Germans.*"

A German who'd worked at Brighton before the war was among several Germans speaking perfect English. He was fed up with the war and wanted it over. A British soldier agreed.

"It was a highly emotional moment," said University of Pennsylvania historian Paul Fussell in 1996. "It's the last gesture of the nineteenth-century idea that human beings are getting better the longer the human race goes on."

If civilisation had a final day, it was Christmas Day, 1914. German officers brought barrels of beer for their men and British soldiers too; the British complained French beer was barely fit to drink. The two forces exchanged gifts and souvenirs: buttons and badges, hats, chocolate bars, tobacco, and tins of processed beef. Men kicked about soccer balls, between swilling tots of rum and showing their family photographs. In the evening, they again sang Christmas carols, with 'Silent Night' the most popular for being known by both sides alike. Before midnight, they wished each other well and returned to their lines.

British and German soldiers refused to resume the war, until their superior officers threatened them with execution (according to Reverend Laurel in conversation with me). "And, then," continued Simkins, "partly because the generals didn't want it to happen, and partly because units moved out of the line and others came in, the thing died away." At eight thirty the day after

Christmas, Captain Stockwell of the Royal Welsh Fusiliers fired three shots into the air and climbed onto his parapet. The officer who'd given him beer the previous day also appeared on the German parapet. They bowed, saluted, and climbed back into their trenches.

A few moments afterwards, Stockwell heard the German fire two shots into the air. "The war," said Stockwell, "was on again."

Far from causing war, our shared race and Christianity stopped it, in places, however briefly. Nothing else brought peace to Europe for almost four more years.

Atheism, agnosticism, and doubts about God so great that what remains can barely be called faith are means of Western peoples trying to separate our individual selves from our cultures and pasts. So is a complete ignorance and indifference beyond mere atheism or agnosticism.

Prompted by Jewish musician Bob Dylan's 1963 song 'With God on Our Side,' we came to mock our forebears fighting wars against each other all thinking God was on their sides, but He was. We weren't. Had the German and British leaderships in 1939 sensed the Christian European commonality their soldiers sensed at Christmas 1914, there'd have been no World War II.

In his autobiography *Sometimes I Forgot to Laugh*, English cricketer and journalist Peter Roebuck said his father lost his Christian faith because he didn't think God could allow the Great War killing to continue. Roebuck killed himself in 2011 by jumping from a Cape Town hotel window, while South African police were questioning him about his sexual assault of a Zimbabwe man.

So often when we ask how God could allow awful things to happen, we could more easily ask it of ourselves. Blaming God for our failings is much easier than blaming ourselves for what we do with our God-given choices. Our races and cultures served us well. The human authorities in whom the masses trusted failed us badly. Our churches and governments, not God or our countries, betrayed us. They did again. They are again.

We might talk of faith in people, but we have no faith in people, not in us. Having lost confidence in ourselves, we found it in everyone else. The indifference to our peoples that sustained war in Europe past 1914 and brought war to Europe in 1939 became individualism. It brought us multiculturalism.

We fear nationalism dragging us to kill and be killed, but that was militarism. The problem wasn't the patriotism of our men marching off to war, but the lack of nationalism among our leaders creating and continuing the carnage.

Walking through the Australian War Memorial in Canberra, the second last day of September 2010, I paused at a particularly haunting model. A life-sized figure of a man sat crestfallen, amidst the devastation of a Great War battlefield. His head was burrowed in his hands. The mud and death couldn't conceal his despair.

My three other children with me that day were elsewhere in the memorial, while standing beside me was my eldest son. Then fourteen years of age, he would've been a few years too young to have been caught up in that most calamitous of wars a century ago. "If you take away the reasons people had for dying," I told him, understanding why we had, "God, King, and Country, then you take away the reasons we have for living."

3. ETERNITY

"People need to understand the value of honouring their ancestors," said Major Sumner, an Aboriginal elder of the Ngarrindjeri people in London in 2009. "They get a little taste of...what we believe in...when they see what is happening in France," he explained, referring to archaeologists in a muddy French field exhuming the bodies of a hundred and ninety Australian soldiers from their Great War graves. They would then receive a military reburial, almost a century after they died. "That is what it is all about, bringing home your people."

Sumner and another elder conducted a traditional Aboriginal smoking ceremony before the bones of several Aborigines, whose remains had been among those of six hundred Aborigines collected centuries earlier by British universities and museums for study. Oxford University's Museum of Natural History in Liverpool had returned the bones for reburial in Australia according to Ngarrindjeri cultural practices. "We are two different cultures," continued Sumner. "We are two different races, and we are the oldest living culture in the world... what is happening in France, people can learn something from that because it is no different at all, really... Wanting to bring home your dead is the same feeling for everyone."

All the races on earth honour their ancestors but ours, save for our military forces. The rest of us empathise for other people's ancestors, but rarely our own: those names born one day to die. Oh, we have our family heirlooms: those tall army boots our grandfathers brought back from the Great War, the sterling silver salt bowls we can't recall who gave us. When the television cameras come, we queue before antique experts to learn their monetary values.

We're no longer peoples, so can't call any people's history ours. They're exercises in academic discourse, interest, or curiosity. We have only personal histories, if we're lucky enough to have kept our old schoolbooks in a box at the back of the garage. They can seem pointless to keep, even for those of us with histories we learnt from the time before we became individuals.

Unwilling to research pasts beyond our own, we have little knowledge beyond light entertainment in films and television programmes. History is a topic for a television documentary we faithfully watch, or occasionally catch if there's nothing better to do. Whatever we see we promptly forget, or confidently impart upon others before soon forgetting.

Without wars to fight, there can be no victories. War was a futile failing. We dishonour our dead.

Few of us notice the memorial poplar trees and lawns our forebears laid to contemplate and honour our war fallen. Fewer still know the reasons our soldiers, sailors, and airmen fought, even if we pause a day or two a year to recall there once were wars. Armistice Day 2010, my second daughter told me the school librarian ushered the children to a minute's silence at eleven o'clock, with her youngest brother's class. The Korean boy Sung Wong remained at his computer; our dead meant nothing to him. If we don't remember our dead, nobody will.

"Our belief is that when our people's remains are not with their people and in our country," said Sumner, "then their spirit is wandering. Unless they going back home, the spirit never rests. These are people that we know are uneasy... there is a lot of unhealthy spirits in our community, all sorts of negative energies around our own people."

I know the feeling. Buried in our parish Anglican church cemetery are some of our nineteenth-century pioneers, when war was for heroes who came home alive. They built them and us a country, with farms, homes, and towns. Their names would be forgotten, but for the names of old streets and suburbs and their burial places.

When they died, their loved ones cast grand graves upon stone slabs with Biblical and other poetic testimonials and devotions, often behind iron palings marking their last plots of land. Stonemasons carved mournful statues of cherubs, angels, and Jesus weeping for their loss. God in eternity made graveyards peaceful places. We loved life more than we feared death.

That was until 1914. Graves laid after the Great War could've been frightening, but lie low on simple stone near the ground without saying very much: brief words of love and loss. So devastated by the carnage, we kicked up our heels in the 1920s trying not to be distracted by the dead. We couldn't bear to think more of death, explained an elderly, burly woman from our local historical society, guiding a group of us exploring the cemetery ninety years after the war ended.

The eleven o'clock walking tour was the second that morning, during the church's anniversary fête; ours is the only church in the municipality with a cemetery. The day was warm; the sky blue and clear. When we tired, we rested on the graves. Shades of black soiled the oldest statues. Dollops of aged fungi melded into rock, providing patterns in the grey. Headstones and other slabs of stone were cracked. Iron palings had rusted. Most of the group was much older than I was; my seven-year-old second son paid little attention to anything said or the graves around us. Just three descendants of people buried there walked with us.

Mavis was the mother of a boy with whom I'd been at school. Bill had died in his sleep, his body left defenceless by the human immunodeficiency virus. Not only wars kill men too young to die.

Our lives since a second great war are an even more reckless abandonment than they were after the first. We've stopped considering death and valuing life.

Large numbers of Asians had come into the area in recent years. Very, very few of them came to our much-too-English church or fête. Only one immigrant was among the more than a dozen people wandering the graves: somebody's part-Asian great-great-something-grandchild: a rare child aside my son.

The tour's theme that year among the graves was mothers and mothering, from the time no honour or fulfilment exceeded bearing and raising a dozen or more children. The mothering recognised the midwives, who tenderly helped the mothers and our civilisation bear children and grow. Our guide talked a little of the lives of people whose names we saw inscribed.

Nineteenth-century parishioners believed cremation prevented us rising from the dead on Judgement Day. Through the twentieth century, less thoughtful generations built a columbarium. It appears to be just a wall between the church and cemetery, but if we stand close enough we see brass plaques in place of holes. Ashes lie in tidy boxes between the reddish-brown bricks and pale mortar, for anybody pausing to peer. Never is death more nondescript.

We still can't bear to think of dying. The concrete beneath

bland brass markers of our deaths we've come to lay, when we lay markers at all, remain innocuous. The graves of all people in that walking tour, including mine, will likely be innocuous. My mother's grave in another cemetery hides below trim lawns with rows of roses and occasional tall trees. Death hides within the names. People who've died hide with it.

The millions fighting the Great War included the obvious cream of our countries' youth, of Europe and her empires. Among the guardians of civilisation were also petty criminals like Arthur Stace, born in the Balmain slums in 1884. A child of alcoholics, Stace followed the family trade and, while still a teenager, became an alcoholic. At the age of fifteen he was in gaol, before finding a new career around illegal gambling dens keeping watch for police. In his twenties, he was a scout for his sisters' brothels. Going to the Great War might've been the noblest thing he'd done, but he was gassed in France and returned to Sydney blind in one eye. Soon an alcoholic again, he progressed through a range of favoured beverages until, run out of money, he took to methylated spirits.

Amidst the Great Depression, free food brought him into the St Barnabas Church hall, Broadway the first Wednesday night of August 1930. Three hundred men, most of them bums, endured a ninety-minute sermon from the Reverend Hammond to earn their meals: the price they paid. Accounts differed as to what happened that night. One said that Stace asked of the well-known criminal beside him, "Who are they?"

"I'd reckon they'd be Christians," the criminal replied. If the account was right then the two men hadn't considered themselves Christian, although their people and country were.

"Well, look at them and look at us," said Stace. "I'm having a go at what they have got." With that, he slipped down on his knees and prayed.

Another account had him hearing the sermon before walking across the road to Victoria Park. Beneath a massive Moreton Bay Fig tree, Stace found his faith.

Whatever happened that night, Stace soon stopped drinking alcohol and obtained a job. Two years later, at the Burton Street Baptist Church in Darlinghurst, he heard a sermon by evangelist John Ridley. What crushed other people's faith hadn't crushed Ridley's; he'd earned a Military Cross in the Great War. The second Monday night of November 1932, Ridley quoted a passage from the Book of Isaiah. "*For thus saith the high and lofty One that inhabiteth Eternity, whose name is Holy; I dwell in the high and holy place, with him also that is of a contrite and humble spirit, to revive the spirit of the humble, and to revive the heart of the contrite ones.*"

"Eternity, Eternity," preached Ridley, "I wish that I could sound or shout that word to everyone in the streets of Sydney. You've got to meet it, where will you spend Eternity?"

The word rang in Stace's ears as he left the church. He began crying. "I had a piece of chalk in my pocket," he said later, "and I bent down there and wrote it. The funny thing is that before I wrote, I could hardly have spelled my own name. I had no schooling and I couldn't have spelt 'eternity' for hundred quid, but it came out smoothly in beautiful copperplate script. I couldn't understand it, and I still can't."

He set about an extraordinary crusade. Year upon year, without revealing his identity, Stace scratched the word "*Eternity*" in chalk and crayon around Sydney footpaths. At first, another fellow followed him around and, with a few careful strokes, changed his writing to "*Maternity*." To prevent that happening, Stace learned to write the opening letter as a capital "*E*" with two bold curves and a tail from the final letter "*y*" to underline it. The word "*Eternity*" in his long, flowing, flowery style became part of a people's folklore: a little shot of character in a city with only a century and a half behind it.

For more than twenty years, Stace's identity was a secret; he wrote in the early morning, before most people appeared. Only when the reverend of the church at which he worked as a cleaner saw him pull out his chalk and write the word was the mystery solved. Stace continued writing. He might've written the word "*Eternity*" half a million times over thirty-five years or so, before dying in a nursing home in 1967.

Thirty-two years after his death, as part of the New Year's Eve fireworks display for the new millennium, the word "*Eternity*" burnt in giant scrolling letters from the Sydney Harbour Bridge. Eighty-one years after the Great War's end, many old buildings had gone. New races occupied the city. Older people who recognised Stace's style drew comfort, when so much else from our heritage had gone. Our eternity was brief.

For Western individuals without thought of time before our solitary little lives or afterwards, eternity is just a word. We believe in words without trying to understand them, however beautifully they're put together or how many times they're written up in lights. Stripped of all the reasons we'd gone to war, we've stripped ourselves. We deny ourselves history and a future: the end of eternity.

Nations, races, and religions afford people the comforts of pasts before our lives began. They afford us hopes of futures after our deaths. Without them, we can't imagine much before yesterday morning or further ahead than a week from Thursday. Our lives are simply instants in time; that's all we have. The world began sometime around our solitary births and will end with our solitary deaths. In our lives without eternity, the Great War never happened. Nothing before our births or recorded memory ever really happened. We care less about our long-dead grandparents than about pushing people aside for better views of fireworks.

For everyone who turns towards the stars or into the veins of a leaf, eternity isn't just a word. It's something more than science about time, extending without limit beyond our individual lives. It's an emotional connection to immeasurable time.

Birds and animals have life and death, but not eternity: a human consciousness that pauses long enough to wonder where we sit in unfathomable space and period. It's time through generations dead and not yet born, through ancient times and peoples not so long ago. It's time before the universe began and after it ends, when the stories of our lives mean everything and mean nothing at all. At eternity, there's only God and people with Him.

Without feeling our ancestral pasts as other races do, we've surrendered our sense of eternity. We've lost our link with our ancestors. Other races retain eternity, offering them religion and peoples but only their own. They have forever for which to fight, defend, and honour. Shining from the Sydney Harbour Bridge for the New Year 2009 were the Chinese symbols for the yin and yang.

Eternity can be comforting, when the past century has pained us. Confined to a world with few ideals and little beauty or romance remaining, we've become the most rabid of cynics. If there's one reason above all others why individualism leaves our lives hollow, people cultureless, and civilisation tenuous, it lies in the momentariness of our existence. Our lives are predicated upon our individual selves, living so much for the moment. We can't possess pasts or futures without feeling ourselves amidst them.

4. RELIGION BY RACE

My mother said she didn't become a Christian. She was born one.

When I was young, I was troubled to know I was Christian for being born of European peoples, however far from Europe I was. If I'd been born of most other races, were such a thing possible, I'd have been of another religion. What I didn't appreciate was that if I'd been born two thousand years earlier, I'd have been polytheistic pagan.

Understanding the West requires us to know something of classical Greece, the Roman Empire, and our religious history. We can't hope to understand curious circles of stones like Stonehenge without knowledge of our history before Christianity.

Christian festivals replaced pagan festivals, but that's no reason to reject Christianity. It's reason to recognise our Christian heritage is a European heritage.

The God of Abraham was a rare single God in ancient times, when religion reflected a natural order of things. Jews can claim the same religion they've always been, as can Africans and American Indians worshipping their ancient spirits. Hindus have a compilation of beliefs (some of them monotheistic) that might reflect ancient origins. Australian Aborigines have their Dreamtime, although our delicate, unquestioning deference doesn't let me know whether they believe giant goannas roamed the desert. They might just enjoy stories.

Other races found new religions. Buddha lived in the sixth and fifth centuries before Christ. Mohammed lived in the sixth and seventh centuries after Christ. Buddhist, Christian, and Muslim peoples all had previous religions.

Romans established colonies throughout Europe, North Africa, and the Middle East in their expanding empire, spreading civilisation. Roman religion filled Roman life, but the people who believed Jupiter was king among many gods allowed other peoples their sects. Each race had its religion, but the Romans persecuted the new Christian religion unfolding in the first years *anno Domini* for purporting to be a religion for everyone, including Romans. Persecution didn't deter Christians from spreading their message.

Greeks who'd invented democracy in about 508 B.C., Before Christ, and believed in Venus among many gods gradually became Christians. Only in 311 and 313, when a tenth of the Roman population was Christian, did the emperors Galerius and Constantine make Christianity legal in Rome and then the empire. Thereafter, all Roman emperors bar one would be Christian. The empire adopted religious hegemony to become the Holy Roman Empire. Her inheritor is the Roman Catholic Church.

Christian saints spread the new faith through Europe, while empires rose and fell. Vikings worshiping Thor and other Scandinavian gods established colonies spreading their people across the North Atlantic, before becoming Christians. The Roman Catholic Church pressed them to cease attacking fellow Christians. Only Christianity among the world's religions enjoyed supranational structures, joining Europeans across nations because Rome had. Common Christianity was a force for peace.

A rare thing uniting Europeans was our sense of being Christian. Swedes were indistinguishable from Spaniards, Greeks from Germans, before God. That remained notwithstanding the rise of the denominations, which mirrored disparate cultures and peoples. Conflict sometimes arose between Roman Catholics and Protestants, because conflicts sometimes arise between peoples over anything they value.

While we colonised the world preaching to other races, our identities forged over more than a thousand and close to two thousand years didn't slip away. Each person's faith or lack of it mattered less than being English, French, and so forth. Thomas Jefferson's home, Monticello, in Virginia was a temple to European thought: a museum within a museum. His Declaration of Independence was an enthusiastic outpouring of the most idyllic ideals he'd learnt from his studies at home and in Europe.

Jefferson called himself Christian, while privately wavering about Jesus' divinity and defying the Church's authority. Some say a handful of other American founding fathers did too. Religious doubt, even disbelief, didn't keep a European from being Christian.

Much is made today of article 11 of the Treaty of Tripoli, 1797. *"As the Government of the United States of America is not, in any sense, founded on the Christian religion; as it has in itself no character of enmity against the laws, religion, or tranquility, of Mussulmen; and as the said States never entered into any war or act of hostility against any Mahometan nation, it is declared by the parties that no pretext arising from religious opinions shall ever produce an interruption of the harmony existing between the two countries."* The Mussulmen were Muslims, Mahometan was Muslim.

Secretary of war James McHenry protested the article before its ratification. *"The Senate, my good friend,"* he wrote in a letter to the secretary of the treasury Oliver Wolcott in September 1800, *"and I said so at the time, ought never to have ratified the treaty alluded to, with the declaration that 'the government of the United States, is not, in any sense, founded on the Christian religion.' What else is it founded on?"*

I suggest the treaty demonstrated the extent to which America sought to avoid religious conflict with Muslim Tripolitania. She failed, with the Pasha of Tripoli breaching the Treaty of Tripoli in 1801. The Treaty of Peace and Amity, which superseded the Treaty of Tripoli in 1805, did not contain the phrase *"not, in any sense, founded on the Christian religion."* We fare better by asserting our culture than denying it.

Europe's cultural heritage is more Christian than anything else: the cultures of Christendom. Although Jefferson wrote in 1814 that Christianity wasn't part of the common law, he may well have referred to belief in the Christian God rather than Christian values and culture. In its 1824 decision in *Updegraph v Commonwealth*, the Pennsylvania Supreme Court held that "Christianity, general Christianity, is, and always has been, a part of the common law of Pennsylvania."

The case was cited in the American Supreme Court decision in the 1892 case of *Church of the Holy Trinity v United States*. "These, and many other matters which might be noticed," remarked Justice Brewer, "add a volume of unofficial declarations to the mass of organic utterances that this is a Christian nation."

America being a Christian nation meant allowing a foreign clergyman to immigrate in that case. It meant refusing to allow a foreign clergyman to immigrate in the 1931 case of *United States v Macintosh*, after he refused to take an oath to bear arms in America's defence unless he believed it to be morally justified. "We are a Christian people," said Justice Sutherland, "according to one another the equal right of religious freedom, and acknowledging with reverence the duty of obedience to the will of God." Obedience to America's laws was "not inconsistent with the will of

God."

Neither case held Christianity to be an official religion or compelled all Americans to believe it. Both cases could have been replicated in any other European or colonial European country at the time; those that weren't Christian *ab initio* had become so. Only Albania had ceased (but it had ceased being European altogether under Turkish rule). We were Christians for being Christian peoples, European, wherever we happened to live. We were religious by birth, born to faith, even if our individual faiths faltered. Our collective Christian identity didn't depend upon personal belief.

Trying to move beyond natural orders of things, collective religious identities ended in the Russian Empire with the coming of communism after World War I. Communism separated Soviet citizens not just from their cultural heritages but from the West.

Collective religious identities ended for the free West after World War II. Not about to foist identity upon anyone, not even ourselves, we increasingly refused to identify with a group not of our choosing.

Conversely, we melded our heritage with the Jews after the Holocaust as we'd never before done, clumsily calling it Judeo–Christian. The West became a Judeo–European fusion neither Jewish nor European.

Jews had no reason to meld their past with ours, and every reason not to. Jewish culture remained Jewish.

Thinking we could compartmentalise our Christianity and other races their religions from everything else, we stopped thinking religion is an aspect of culture and culture an aspect of religion. We reduced religion to a matter of personal faith, which we each have or we don't.

Yet, the Universal Declaration of Human Rights, which the United Nations General Assembly adopted in 1948, distinguished religion from belief, while recognising their common correlation. "*Everyone has the right to freedom of thought, conscience and religion,*" provided article 18, "*this right includes freedom to change his religion or belief, and freedom, either alone or in community with others and in public or private, to manifest his religion or belief in teaching, practice, worship and observance.*"

For the most part, we'd long enjoyed the right to change religion without thinking of taking it up, much as we'd long enjoyed the rest of what we'd come to call human rights. What we began to lose after World War II was the sense that religion was also our inheritance. Religion became only something we chose, our individual decision to make, much like varieties of ice cream from a stall. We focused upon being free to change our religion and abandon religion altogether, without appreciating the cultural heritage by which we began with a religion. What we choose, we can choose to refuse.

Presumably that means people of other races are also free to choose and change their religion, although we're not so rude as to mention it. We've ceased to see religion as a means to salvation, just as it failed to be for Jews alighting from trains into Birkenau. The God of Moses not being real for Jews, we think He can't be real for us.

Merely because we treat religion in such a passing manner doesn't mean other races see their religion, or ours, the same way. For most of them, there's more to religion than what people per chance believe. Religion remains something to which people are born: their race's cultural identity. My Hong Kong Chinese friend Ted spent some small time in the St James Anglican Church, Turramurra. When his mother died, he returned to Hong Kong for their traditional Chinese and Buddhist rituals.

Race determines religion (when the West thinks we have neither). Personal belief is something else altogether. A Muslim Iranian woman at our parish Anglican church said Iran is rife with people not believing in god. Religion being important, Islam fills their lives nevertheless. We'd call them atheist or agnostic, but they don't call themselves that. They're Muslims, who don't talk of faiths lapsing as we've come to talk of Christian faiths lapsing. They dwell upon their collective identity, instead of individual faith. To be Persian is to be Muslim. Race and religion aren't readily distinguished.

Pakistan's definition as much by religion as race doesn't determine what each Pakistani's faith should mean. Cricketer Imran Khan reputedly enjoyed a quiet drink of alcohol and ate during daylight hours in Ramadan, while being a Muslim of faith.

Race and religious identity remain wrapped together for Jews. To be a Jew is to be Jewish; Jews are Jews whatever their faith. From race came their religion.

Identity matters more than belief; the distinction can be

profound. Faiths or faithlessness are there to select, but identities don't change because a person's beliefs change, or change again. Faiths lapse, identities don't.

Religious identities reflect racial identities, subordinate to them, much as they once did for us. Buddhists don't identify with Buddhists of other races. Islam becoming the Arabs' and Persians' religion unites them only in conflicts with others. Any Islamic caliphate divides along racial lines.

Religious and racial loyalties we're quick to blame for wars. They're reasons for other races not to kill each other.

We optimistically called the rioting and revolution through the Middle East in 2011 the Arab Spring, so certain were we that Arabs are like us, but Arabs are as much Muslims as Arabs: god and country are the same. Only tribe means more than country. After the Gaddafi regime ordered the Libyan Army to attack the town of Zliten, close to Misrata, amidst the 2011 Libyan Civil War, Colonel Wissam Miland defected to the rebels. "I thought it was wrong to kill Muslims and fellow Libyans," he said, "but if I refused the order I would be shot immediately, so I decided to surrender."

Most of the world remains so racially and religiously homogenous that religious identity doesn't require paperwork, or too disorganised to do anything about it, but identification papers in Egypt specify a person's religion. In 2010, Minority Rights Group International complained that Egypt limited the options to Islam, Christianity, and Judaism, because members of the nineteenth-century Persian sect Baha'i couldn't get identification papers. They thus couldn't work or access healthcare.

Malaysian birth certificates specify a baby's religion. Malaysian law declares Malays to be born Muslim. The National Fatwa Council decreed that a child is born Muslim if either parent is Muslim, whatever the other parent happens to be and the parents happen to think. Malaysian Muslims may renounce their religion, without denying that Islam is the religion to which they were born.

In 2010, a senior teacher at St Thomas Primary School (funnily enough) caned ten-year-old Basil ten times across the hand for eating a meal (fried rice and pork, prepared by his Christian mother, Angela Jabing) that wasn't halal. The boy's birth certificate omitted his religion but he was raised a Christian after his father, Beginda Minda, renounced being a Muslim in 1999, before the boy was born. The problem for Basil was his father standing as a

Muslim candidate in elections in 1999 and 2004. The issue was important enough for the Malaysian parliament to debate.

Apostasy is the renunciation of a person's religion. Islam doesn't normally recognise Muslims renouncing their faith; the Islamic world expands more readily than it contracts. Muslim countries such as Saudi Arabia, Mauritania, and the Comoros make apostasy punishable by death, at least for Muslims. Judaism and Christianity allow apostasy. Christians in the West find it almost compulsory.

The races we allow into our countries continue the ways of their race, never too good at being what we want them to be or insist they already are. That's no less the case for the few adopting new faiths. Attending our parish Anglican church is Richard, always dressed in a suit and with an accent hinting of upper-class British in spite of being Indian. His Indian friends continued calling him Hindu after he'd adopted Christianity.

Rejecting our faith doesn't require us to reject our religion. The March to May 2009 edition of *Creation* magazine reported receiving indignant correspondence from people calling themselves atheist Christians. Atheism was merely an adjective, much as the lack of belief we call agnosticism can be. The noun was being a Christian. They identified with Christianity.

We might think that's bizarre, but we were Christian countries and peoples for centuries without us all sharing the faith. We identified as Christians or a Christian denomination because our people did, without dwelling upon what we individually believed. We had atheists and agnostics, although fewer than now, while Christianity was inextricably a feature of our provincial, national, and European identities. Western peoples without faith gave up calling themselves Christian through the twentieth century because they gave up calling themselves European.

We no longer dwell on what religion might mean, but in the parlance of identity being the noun and belief merely an adjective, Richard at our parish Anglican church is a Christian Hindu. It makes for betwixt and between people, but if religion were merely belief and belief was identity, then Richard would have lost his identity becoming Christian. He didn't. Losing faith, finding it, or finding it anew doesn't alter identities. Peoples don't change because a person takes up the faith or leaves it.

5. ENLIGHTENMENT

Some in my philosophy club meeting the third Wednesday of July 2010 in Shelly's bookshop, when we explored *Discourse on the Method* and *Meditations on First Philosophy*, believed the seventeenth-century French philosopher René Descartes initiated Europe's Age of Enlightenment. "*Je pense donc je suis*," he wrote. For a while there, my French friend Patrick repeated it in Latin, "*Cogito ergo sum*," at the end of every electronic mail message he sent. "I doubt, therefore I think, therefore I am."

Descartes' was a peculiarly European philosophy; the Enlightenment was ours. The Age of Enlightenment asserted individuals thinking independently of each other, of individuality, but remained an age of races and religion. Descartes didn't cease being French for doubting and thinking, not even in Latin, or living and dying in the court of the Queen of Sweden.

Christianity shaped many of our values and attitudes. From its inception, Christianity offered people choice to believe. Those choices have consequences. In spite of the Church's criticism of some of Descartes' writing, the devout Roman Catholic believed that perfect human existence, by virtue of a questioning mind, proved the existence of a perfect God. Only something perfect could create something perfect, he reasoned.

Since the Great War, we've ceased believing in perfect human existence. We thus either cease believing in God or dwell upon our sins.

Christianity drew upon science, including the science from times before Christ. Among the stone figures of the Chartres Cathedral are images from ancient Greece and Rome, including Pythagoras.

Artistic romanticism and scientific reason came together from the late eighteenth through the nineteenth and early twentieth centuries with our sense of God controlling a logically consistent, divine universe. Without a god or gods, there's no logical reason why the sun should rise in the east tomorrow simply because it rose there today and every day past. Our faith in God's order underpinned Western science.

Other races had knowledge, but not the laws of physics and other sciences we discovered. A German friar, Gregor Mendel, founded modern genetics with experiments upon plants from 1854. A Belgian priest, George Lemaître, developed what became known as the Big Bang Theory in 1927. Many great achievements were born from Europe, as we learn when we take chances to check.

Our Age of Enlightenment is passed. We have multiculturalism instead.

When our conversation turned to religion at the Association of Corporate Counsel drinks the penultimate Wednesday in July 2015, a legal recruiter Steven expressed his atheism by saying that he believed in science. I responded, "So do I." People cite science supposedly to refute our religion, Christianity, without troubling themselves to learn either the science or Christianity.

Our schools haven't just stopped teaching Biblical stories. They've forbidden it. Doing so in the name of science claimed Christianity was unscientific, but Creationism, Noah's flood, and so forth aren't just Biblical stories. They're also Muslim and Jewish stories, for the history until Abraham all three religions believe. What we slander about Christians would be insensitive to Muslims, so teachers in Britain who denounce Christian children's beliefs about Creation don't challenge the same beliefs among Muslim children.

"*The Muslim philosophy of science is based on the idea that God is the creator of everything,*" said the booklet *Learning from One Another: Bringing Muslim Perspectives into Australian Schools.* "*Science in this case is driven and inspired by divine revelation, not simply questioning or investigating everything.*"

Christianity questioned and investigated everything. Islam proudly does not.

American comedian George Carlin criticised many aspects of religion, but appreciated his education at the Corpus Christi School, Manhattan. "They gave me the tools to reject my faith," he said in 1995. "They taught me to question and think for myself and to believe in my instincts, to such an extent that I just said, 'This is a wonderful fairy tale they have going here, but it's not for me.'"

Western antagonism towards Christianity was never about science. If it were, then a teacher wouldn't have given one particular task for assessment to my eldest son's class in first term, year nine. The subject wasn't cultural studies or even religion but geography, which I'd previously imagined was science, but there are no sciences in our multicultural vision. There's only ideology, without questioning or investigation. The children's assignment was to describe the earth's creation from the viewpoint of the Aboriginal Dreamtime.

The West no longer tolerates the suggestion God's hands created anything, not our God. Our postmodern perspective we call human rights was the weapon to wind back Christianity from Italy in 2009, when the European Court of Human Rights banned crucifixes from Italian classrooms. It made the unremarkable observation that crucifixes "could reasonably be associated with Catholicism."

The Strasbourg court believed that a crucifix was "disturbing for pupils who practised other religions or were atheists, particularly if they belonged to religious minorities." What was so disturbing about Christianity wasn't made clear, but hadn't needed to be since the Holocaust. According to the court, crucifixes restricted "the right of children to believe or not to believe," although when children are no longer taught about God, their only right is not to believe. What the court called "educational pluralism" is our euphemism for banning Western cultures. We're too sensitive to maintain them.

In 2011, the Strasbourg court reversed its decision, because there was no evidence the crucifixes in classrooms could influence children. That made them acceptable.

Yet all the court decisions affirmed (if only inadvertently) that Western identity encompasses Christianity, with national identities no less Christian for being Christian denominations. The Italian court in Veneto in first instance refused to ban the crucifixes from schools because, by the twenty-first century, they were no longer so much a religious symbol but "the symbol of Italian history and culture, and consequently of Italian identity."

On the 2010 mining industry Christmas cruise whiling around Sydney Harbour, I approached geologist Ian Plimer. Sixteen years earlier, in 1994, Plimer criticised Christian beliefs and literal interpretations of the Bible in his book *Telling Lies for God: Reason vs. Creationism*. He also sued researcher Allen Roberts alleging Roberts' theories on the location of Noah's Ark were misleading and deceptive advertising under the Trade Practices Act 1974. Plimer lost.

(He had a point about Biblical interpretation. The Bible isn't always a text to read precisely, like a recipe book. Traditionally, information wasn't conveyed in such terms. It's a literary work, by which the poet mightn't mean every phrase to be literally true, simply because it is true.

Do the people who smugly criticise the Bible really think that nobody else in two thousand years asked how people could exist if Adam and Eve had only two sons, one of whom killed the other? Every challenge to the Bible has long been answered, for anyone interested in scholarship. God creating the universe matters more than whether He took seven days doing so.)

Plimer described himself to me as being a spiritual agnostic, essentially because he felt the existence of God was unknowable. Expecting a debate, I put to him that being a Christian could be a matter of identity instead of only belief. He surprised me not just by agreeing with me, but by rushing into a litany of greatness in our Western culture attributable to Christianity.

Most of it, like our political and legal systems, I'd already heard and realised. Christian Europe invented human rights, giving more rights to more people than any other race or religion, even if we've made a mess of them since the Second World War. We invented individuality, individualism, and their excesses. We produced the liberal democracies, even if we fail miserably to defend them.

I later learned of a similar stance from atheist Richard Dawkins, author of *The God Delusion*. He called himself a cultural Christian. Religion being so much of a culture, retaining our connection to our collective religion is retaining our connection to our culture. Plimer and Dawkins recognised their heritage better than many Western people of faith.

According to the Book of Genesis, failing to help their poor was among the sins causing God to destroy the cities of Sodom and Gomorrah (where most sights would be immediately recognisable in many a modern metropolis). Going much further than other religions, Western Christianity taught us to help other peoples as well as our own: giving is better than receiving. Without Christianity, we ceased speaking of sin, but retained our enthusiasm to help others. At least we go some way towards helping our poor. Generous is a Western thing to be, if not always with each other.

While we condemn so much of our past European practice and thought, we shy away from condemning the political and economic legacies of our Age of Enlightenment: liberalism and free market economics. Both are predicated upon people making choices and making different choices.

We can't expunge our Christian culture without losing something of our European culture. Britons don't need to be religious to lament that, by 2010, some toyshops no longer sold pigs in their animal sets for fear of offending Muslims and Jews. We needn't attend church to appreciate nativity scenes in shopping centre windows and Christmas carols, if not for us then for our children.

We know the right to traditions, because we accord it to others. We no longer demand it for ourselves.

We reject priority for Christianity in our countries because we reject priority for our cultures, even if we've personally kept the faith. Around 1990, former New South Wales Liberal Party leader John Dowd told my friend Stephen that Australia was no longer Christian.

"Whatever we once were," senator Barack Obama told a Call to Renewal conference the last Wednesday in June 2006, describing America, "we are no longer a Christian nation – at least, not just. We are also a Jewish nation, a Muslim nation, a Buddhist nation, and a Hindu nation, and a nation of non-believers." He repeated the sentiment many times, most pointedly on a visit to Muslim Turkey in the first year of his presidency. (Turkey never called itself a Christian nation, even when twenty percent of its population was Christian.) Obama at least acknowledged America had been a Christian nation. Others, including my Jewish friend Harry, insist she never was.

What made Obama's words unusual was listing other religions that America was, but a country claiming contradictory religions isn't any. It isn't a nation, but a whopping patch of land on which different races and their religions happen to be.

Other Western countries call themselves secular, which doesn't mean immigrant races identify less with their religions. It means we don't identify with ours.

The Koran and Old Testament set out disciplines and practices particular to the region (amidst matters of morality also recorded there). Most obvious are their rules about food, including the prohibition upon eating shellfish in the Book of Leviticus. (In the first century, Roman philosopher Pliny the Elder wrote that *"shellfish are the prime cause of the decline of morals and the adaptation of an extravagant lifestyle."* Perhaps the prohibition on shellfish was really a prohibition upon extravagant lifestyles, so that shellfish are fine to eat when they're commonplace.)

Hinduism prohibits killing cows. Many Hindus interpret Rig Veda as prohibiting them from drinking cow's milk.

European Christianity never decreed rules about food, although encompassed minor disciplines. They included forsaking the eating of meat on Fridays and through Lent.

Not only won't Muslims or Jews eat pork, they won't eat food from kitchens where pork is served for fear the food is contaminated. In 2014, almost two hundred Subway restaurants in Britain responded to Muslim sensitivities by removing ham and bacon from their menus.

South-eastern Europeans who suffered Turkish rule for centuries aren't as obliging as are other Europeans. Macedonians treasure pork for having been a means of their survival, complaining as the rest of us don't when Liverpool City Council in Sydney omitted pork from the menu for its first Christian Orthodox interfaith lunch in 2015. The menu was corrected, although preparing the meals separately so not to upset Muslims and Jews added great cost to the council in providing the lunch. In 2012, the people of Liverpool had elected Ned Mannoun, a Muslim Lebanese, the mayor.

We'll fund pretty well anything to accommodate other races and religions. For the City of Monash in Melbourne in 2011, the cost of religious pluralism was up to forty-five thousand dollars to install curtains so Muslim women had privacy during female-only exercise classes addressing issues such as "obesity, social isolation, and lack of physical strength," after Muslim women refused to use the pool during normal hours without a privacy screen. The council sought funding from the Victorian Multicultural Commission.

Multiculturalism requires social regulation. Accommodating Muslims led Greater Dandenong City Council to seek approval from the Victorian Civil and Administrative Tribunal to ban uncovered shoulders and thighs for those attending a family event at a swimming pool. The tribunal approved special exercise classes for women at the Clayton Community Centre every second Sunday evening. Women-only programmes operated at public swimming pools at Monash University, Dandenong Oasis recreation centre, and the Don Tatnell Leisure Centre in Parkdale.

For the West to imagine Muslims without sharia is fanciful. What do they do? Believe in Allah and his one true prophet Mohammed but disregard their teachings?

England's first university college founded on secularity, University College London, allowed the Islamic Education and Research Academy to convene a debate "Islam versus Atheism" on the second Saturday in March, 2013. Professor Laurence Krauss agreed to participate because the Muslims promised there'd be no segregation in the audience, but Muslim promises to infidels aren't promises. Muslims honour Allah, the rights of Allah we might say, much as our forebears honoured God. On the night, men and women were kept strictly apart, until Krauss threatened to leave.

Finally drawing a line to defend secularity, the college banned the Islamic academy. *"Given IERA's original intentions for a segregated audience we have concluded that their interests are contrary to UCL's ethos,"* it said in a statement, *"and that we should not allow any further events involving them to take place on UCL premises."*

Conscience is a Western concept, attributable to classical Greece and thence Christianity. Trying to be post-Christian, the West remains Christian in what remains of our culture: a somewhat Christian Western culture, quite distinct from questions about God.

White people hold dear our Christian European presumptions and perspectives long after their faiths have left them. Alan, a fellow student at law school, said the homosexual atheists he encountered who'd been Roman Catholic thought differently to those who'd been Protestant. In particular, lapsed Roman Catholics suffered more feelings of guilt than lapsed Protestants.

Post-Christian atheists come from a different place not just to adherents of other religions but to other atheists. Western atheism is a post-Christian atheism. If there should be a post-Muslim Islam, and there might never be, then it will be as culturally removed from the post-Christian West and post-Jewish Jewry as Islam, Christianity, and Judaism are apart, however much we focus on whatever we think makes them the same. We've become too insular to notice how different we are, but atheistic diversity is no less diversity.

White atheists might find the only way they can live in the

secular state they want is to live among fellow European peoples, faithfully Christian or not. Being a Christian country is a safeguard to the faithful and faithless, and not simply for the glasses of wine. We can think whatever we want to think.

We don't need to be Christian to acknowledge the good things that our compatriots' beliefs in a loving, consistent God bring not just believers but all of us. Not every Christian is about to conquer the Americas, any more than every Muslim is preparing to lay siege on Vienna or every Buddhist is ready to set fire to himself.

White people wanting to live in a Christian country are surely no different to other races wanting to live with their religions. If we're to have the same rights then it becomes beholden on our countries to be Christian, if not in faith then in cultures and laws. In 2010, the *American Catholic* magazine listed thirteen reasons that sharia is incompatible with the American Constitution. They included the reduced weight given testimony from women, and the possible exclusion of testimony from non-Muslims against a Muslim.

Also that year, Shakira Hussein, Islamic researcher at the University of Melbourne, said religious minorities in Islamic countries are particularly vulnerable to accusations of blasphemy by neighbours or family members bearing grudges. That can't be any better for Western atheists and agnostics.

It's all very well for Canada and Britain to offer sharia to matters between Muslims, but why should sharia not also apply to relations between Muslims and others? Subjecting a Muslim to Western laws but not us to sharia is discriminatory. Multiculturalism condemns us to irresolvable conflicts.

The compromises of today become the injustices of tomorrow, as we keep raising other races' expectations. At some point, either we assert our cultures in our countries or we capitulate.

6. VANISHING US

Western countries had national identities, or several of them. Australians wore bush hats that, on men, became slouch hats in war. Canadians were tall mounted policemen with bright, bold red jackets: Dudley Do Right. Canadian women were just as stoic and hardy. Americans were cowboys, cowgirls, or square-jawed marines.

Lots of great culture wasn't Australasian, American, or Canadian. There was English, Scottish, Irish, and Welsh. If Americans were businessmen, then the English were shopkeepers. Englishmen played darts, Englishwomen sewed. Irishmen and women sang ditties. The Welsh sang hymns. Scotsmen donned kilts, Scotswomen their tartan skirts. They danced to the sounds of the pipes; we all had dances to share and games to play.

We had regional identities within our national identities: Cockney rhyming slang, the Hillbillies. They were us and almost us: characters among us.

Frenchmen wore berets, played boules, and drank hot chocolate from a bowl. Frenchwomen were glamorous, even while chewing on croissants with thick serves of jam. Our national foods and beverage were those our people liked most; different peoples liked different things. New Zealanders farmed lambs, Argentinians beef. Germans brewed beer, and no women were more beautiful than the buxom, blonde wenches serving it.

That so many of us weren't like our caricatures didn't matter. They were collectively us, if not individually us, exuding our community traits in long-day festivals and fairs. We were inventors, scientists, artists, and engineers: some more so than others. Whatever one of us did well enough, we claimed for our countries. Every Englishwoman tending to her green garden was matron of the Chelsea Flower Show.

Women's dress sense was elegant and beautiful. Its details changed over time and between ethnicities and climates.

When we weren't distinctive by country or region we were

distinctively European. City men dressed much the same and wore much the same hats.

We were pastors, soldiers, miners, and nurses, sharing manners and mores. If not what we did, then we knew what we should do.

Rituals and celebrations afforded us structure and fun. They included those commemorating lives beginning, coming of age, joining with another, and passing.

Ours weren't monocultures. From her education at Kincoppal, with its rock-carved chapel and castle-like buildings, my mother treasured her schoolgirl studies of French art all her life. I learnt of the Lorelei in my schoolboy studies of German. Cosmopolitanism meant embracing the best of all Europe.

Anglophiles loved England and the English. There was never a word for loving old Ireland, but love her we did. Australians loved Australia, New Zealanders New Zealand. Americans loved America, Canadians Canada, and Quebecois Quebec. We loved each other, we European peoples, and ourselves. Our love has waned since 1914, slumping with every world war.

I think I convinced the two Scotsmen with whom I discussed Scottish independence at a hotel in Alton in 1997 that separating Scotland from the United Kingdom made no sense without escaping the European Union, but the Scottish nationalist movement espoused the former without the latter in the 2014 and '16 referenda. Sometime around the former, I realised that Scottish independence had less to do with the love of Scotland I share than with antagonism to England I don't.

How else could the Scottish Nationalist Party make Humza Yousaf justice secretary in 2018? In 2020, he introduced the Hate Crime and Public Order (Scotland) Bill to the Scottish Parliament. In October 2020, he said he wanted Scots arrested for inciting hatred in their conversations over the dinner table at home, by which he included criticising immigrants.

By the twenty-first century, words of loving Europe and Europeans have faded from use. Instead, we bandy about a lengthening list of alleged phobias of other races and religions, although they're normally just white people caring about their own. Those without fear of our subsuming either don't care or welcome it.

Anglophiles became racists, unless the England of old pubs, thatched cottages, and cobblestone streets is doused with curry powders and Rastafarian reggae. Being a Francophile became Islamaphobic if France is a picnic discussing philosophy with Merlot and cheese, unless we picture North Africans there. We have more words taunting white people for what they supposedly fear, than for what we happen to love.

Our national identities are no longer premised upon people. That would be racist.

They're premised upon anything else. When my wife led our daughters and other girl guides to an Australian citizenship ceremony the first Thursday of October 2010, the girls received colouring sheets denoting the country. There were no Australian homesteads, red-brick houses, or tucker boxes. Nor were there bridges we'd built, clothes lines we'd designed, or songs we had written. Instead, there was an emu, kangaroo, cockatoo, and two koala bears.

One bear I could've understood, but two? It was Australia without Australians: citizenship with animals. It wasn't our country. That was the idea.

We've become countries without people. The Australian identity is one animal or another, the New Zealand a bird that can't fly. They're not even a zoo; our people built zoos. If New Zealand isn't a bird, it's a fern. Canada is a maple leaf: not a whole tree, just a leaf. America is a flurry of stars and stripes, unless someone's offended. Europe is simply the stars.

Our people total to nought. Immigrants are coming to unoccupied land, *terra nullius*, as we no longer consider Australia to have been before we came.

The people we colonial Europeans make pre-eminent in our new national identities are indigenous: Aboriginal stockmen, Maori warriors, Eskimo fishermen, and American Indians. They survive as identities, often without feathers in their hair or other cultural traits. The Aboriginal could as easily be governor-general, the Maori a paediatrician, the Eskimo an ambassador to Bhutan. In their traditional lifestyle, American Indians can't be motifs for an American gridiron team without controversy, as the Washington Redskins can vouch.

We treat their cultures with great deference and humility, without critiquing them as we critique our own. That made it easy for opponents of a bridge to Hindmarsh Island, South Australia in 1994, when Aboriginal women on the island claimed that the bridge would interfere with their "secret women's business." A compliant Australian government barred the building of the bridge, without being so disrespectful as to ask what the secret business was or how a bridge could affect it.

The phrase became part of the popular lexicon. Reuben, the Holyman Limited finance director, described certain directors gathering outside formal board meetings as carrying on "secret men's business."

Other Aboriginal women denied there was any secret women's business, saying men concocted it to stop the bridge being built. A royal commission agreed, but when white Australian property owners sued the government for twenty million dollars they claimed to have lost because of its intervention to stop the building of the bridge, the Federal Court wasn't satisfied that the secret women's business was fabricated. The property owners lost. The saga was a shambles.

The National Parks and Wildlife Service brochure included several interesting tours for the Summer Discovery Programme of 2010 and '11. Three tours were under the heading *"Cultural Heritage,"* but they were all Aboriginal. Without anybody asking, Australian British culture had ceased to exist. It was as if British Australia never existed, even in tours. Ours are the cultures we no longer recall.

We're not altogether sure what culture means anymore, and most of all what our cultures were before other races came and colonial Europeans embraced indigenous cultures. If we're not presuming our past was a time of an ugly one culture, we're presuming we had no culture at all. What we don't denigrate, we deny.

Other races know what their cultures are, without feeling a need to define them. We know their cultures, too. Incas and Aztecs had their cities and temples, Mayans their calendar.

Japanese have Geisha girls and gardens, along with homes like the one reproduced on a hilltop in Cowra. It was easy to forget, as my eldest three children and I moseyed around in 2012, the Australians killed by Japanese in Cowra during World War II. (My eldest son hated the word "mosey.")

We don't know the details, but are happy to accept there are a myriad of Asian, African, American Indian, Aboriginal, and Islander cultures. We're reminded often enough about Indian dancing. Africans have headdresses and dancing. Arabs have sheikhs, camels, and belly dancing, which my friend Megan took up early in the 1990s. Our parish Anglican church hall played host to South American Zumba dance classes, my wife reported in August 2011. We dance other peoples' dances.

To talk of Western cultures, we founder. We reduce the Swiss to being bankers, Germans to making fast cars, Italians to driving them. We have no meaningful understanding of Portuguese, Polish, or Bulgarian cultures.

Only commerce and the world it creates survive: English pubs, Irish pubs. Scandinavian culture becomes ice cream, for anyone to make and everyone to buy. The French speak of culture they're so keen to protect, but struggle to speak of more than cuisine and small farms begging for government subsidy. The last of our selves are whatever's sold in cafés and restaurants, along with keepsakes for tourists. Never did I see more cuckoo clocks than in Switzerland souvenir shops.

Our only certainty is that culture encompasses eating other people's food and drinking anyone's beverage. We of the West aren't the only people to enjoy food and drink. We are the only ones to dwell so much upon them. Eating and drinking take up inordinate amounts of our lives.

We laugh at the food of our forebears; meat pies have become positively uncouth. (My younger children and I are uncouth.) My wife served fairy bread to our children's birthday parties.

Companies so cavalier about immigration can lose from the loss of our cultures. Kraft Foods found that immigrants don't eat the iconic Australian spread Vegemite, although it's careful not to complain.

When black American television host Oprah Winfrey visited Australia in 2010 with all the pomp and media of a Royal Tour, the *Daily Telegraph* newspaper reported the billionairess' *"desire to taste how real Aussies live."* She thus ate barbecued chicken kebabs with tabbouleh and salad.

We'd become so used to living other people's cultures, we needed Trish of Queensland to point out that *"a good Aussie bbq consists of beef, not tabouleh and chicken kebabs."* So far removed are we from any sense of our culture, Woolworth's supermarkets Easter Inspirations recipes in 2014 included Asian-style roast chicken salad and Vietnamese beef wraps.

My wife drinks tea with milk and sugar, as Australian women do. Drinking tea without them as I learnt to drink tea in China didn't make black tea British, any more than it made me Chinese.

If Collingwood Football Club president Eddie McGuire had described western Sydney as the "land of falafel" in 2011 to be a drawcard to the area, there'd have been applause; minister for western Sydney David Borger convened a press conference inviting McGuire to dinner. Instead, McGuire was explaining why he thought recruits to the Greater Western Sydney football team would tire of living there.

A day later, McGuire tried to extricate himself from the outcry by saying he'd meant the term as one of endearment. "These things just get out of control," he said. "If this is now seen to be abusive to the western suburbs, then I apologise to every person in the western suburbs." Nobody cares about criticisms without racial inferences. "Every time I pick up a Sydney newspaper, they refer to Melbourne as bleak city. No one tears up their nighty. Relax."

If we had the self-respect other races enjoy, we'd respect our cuisines more than we do. Not only could we still eat caramel ice cream cake in Cahill's restaurants, we could make them at home with thick caramel sauce, golden sponge cakes, and Streets ice cream from supermarkets.

Milk bars serving milkshakes in cold metal beakers aren't just my fond memories. They're a culture we've let be subsumed. At least my children enjoyed the Acropole in Bathurst; Greeks kept offering that one as Asians are not.

Our food and beverage were whatever enough of us made and consumed: much more than Christmas pudding and Easter eggs, even thick steaks and hot fish and chips. Monasteries produced wonderful wines, breweries bubbled beers. We think ours is the wine of the world, the puddings of all people.

I like lasagne more than laksa, as I like roast lamb with a supple mint sauce. The freshest veal I've eaten was the Wiener schnitzel at the Lion's Pride steakhouse in Dubbo, but too long has passed since I last ate roast beef with Yorkshire pudding. Black Stump steak restaurants ceased operations years ago; the one in which I ate dinner the last night I saw my mother became the site of a noodle bar I never entered, before hosting a Lebanese restaurant.

There was a British culture, not just of beer; culture is much more than just food and beverage. We had pretty, peaceful gardens much softer than those in Japan, villages with fêtes and bring-and-buy sales. Irish sang in pubs in Galway in 1986.

Before becoming so fussed about stereotypes defying our individualism, whatever beliefs and behaviours were common to enough of us but not the rest of the world was our culture. They comprised all that cultures can be, for good and for bad. Our problem is: we feel only the bad.

Catching yabbies in creeks was never sophisticated, but nobody minded. A few friends of mine celebrated their twenty-first birthdays with bush dances, but the only one I've seen through the last thirty years was the old folk of our family Uniting church. Saturday night dances at the Petersham Town Hall were legendary I was told, before I was lucky enough to attend one in 1988. They've long gone, so passé, as other people's dances are not.

Fellow Western cultures fare no better than ours. The area around Liverpool Street had been the Spanish Quarter of Sydney: a small space of paella and flamenco music. By 2009, it was almost gone, subsumed by Chinese property developers for more of their hotels, restaurants, and apartment blocks. "We're seeing a transformation of the Spanish Quarter into Chinatown," observed real estate agent John Bowie Wilson.

After years of falling membership and boardroom divisions, the Spanish Club was selling all but one floor of its two properties. The six Galician immigrant families had grown old, as other European peoples have grown old. They blamed the Spanish Quarter's passing on the Sydney City Council's failure to support them. (It was busy worrying about Aborigines.)

The rest of the West is no more profound. I've not visited Canada, but Canadians and New Zealanders insist, first and foremost, upon not being Americans and Australians. By 2013, Hongcouver referred to the Hong Kong hybrid culture overwhelming Canadian Vancouver.

Watching extracts of films, cartoons, and television programmes we label racist, I'm struck by the sense that racism has come to include linking any cultural trait (such as bowing) to a race. The alien character Jar Jar Binks in three *Star Wars* films was criticised less for being such an irritant than for sounding Jamaican. We're supposed to speak with the same voice and be so much the same. Only white people have accents.

For Australia Day 2010, Macquarie University phoneticians

Felicity Cox and Sallyanne Palethorpe wanted to record Australian accents because they're dying out in the face of multiculturalism. We've no sense of preserving our culture among people, just recording it to tuck into university archives.

Growing up, I called "Cooee" to get my neighbours' attention. I don't hear it from present-day children.

Our ambivalence to our language was a clear contrast with reports from China a few months later that television stations were being directed to avoid the use of English-language abbreviations. "If we don't pay attention and…take measures to stop mixing Chinese with English, the Chinese language won't remain pure in a couple of years," said Huang Youyi, editor in chief of the China International Publishing Group.

The West isn't so interested in purity, not of our cultures. We prefer other people's cultures.

7. MULTICULTURALISM

Multiculturalism expresses the West's determination to embrace other races and religions that began with our embracing of Jews after the Holocaust. Instead of our culture, we value multiculturalism, but multiculturalism isn't a culture or collection of cultures. It's an ideology.

Interracial immigrants, even fellow Europeans we presumed would assimilate, don't defer to our cultures. *"We as Liberals are committed to encouraging and supporting diversity in our multicultural society,"* wrote Petro Georgiou, while a young adviser to Australia's Prime Minister Malcolm Fraser in the late 1970s. Born in Greece, it would've been nice if Georgiou had been more respectful to the people who gave him a home, but there is no multicultural society. *"We reject the sterile Anglo-conformity of past days."* (It's hard to imagine Robert Menzies, who three decades earlier founded the Liberal Party that Fraser later led, saying as much.)

Assimilation having failed across races, interracial immigration demands multiculturalism. We colonised the world to spread civilisation, but came to imagine other races colonising our countries to civilise us.

In 1979, Fraser launched a multicultural television station, the Special Broadcasting Service. One commentator enthused it would civilise us, while the long-standing government television station sought to Anglicise us (for the amount of its British programming) and the commercial stations sought to Americanise us (for the amount of their American programming). The only British, American, or Australian programmes on the new station were about immigrants.

The theme was becoming consistent through the West: civilisation isn't ours, but everyone else's. It comes through television.

When we celebrate the coming of multiculturalism, we celebrate other people's cultures. Acknowledging there could be multiculturalism requires recognition of differences between cultures. Embracing it requires the sense that ours alone was inadequate. When we talk of other cultures enriching us, we're calling our cultures poor by comparison.

We call our countries multicultural, but ours is Western multiculturalism. We know and care little about countries' laws and practices outside the West, even while ambling there on holidays. If we ever looked there with more than a menu in mind, we'd see multiculturalism is rare.

In 2014, the Saudi Arabian interior ministry threatened to deport any of its nine million foreign residents publicly eating, drinking, or smoking during Ramadan. "*They are not excused for being non-Muslim*," said the ministry in a statement, "*anyone living in this country should follow the laws of the Kingdom, including respecting religious sentiments.*"

That meant Muslim sentiments. In 2015, Saudi Arabia introduced ten-year-gaol terms for anyone celebrating Christmas. Singing a Christmas carol or wishing a friend "Merry Christmas" became punishable with a thousand lashes.

A bombed Italian-built Roman Catholic cathedral remains a city landmark in Mogadishu, but in 2013 and 2015, Somalia banned public celebrations of Christmas. "All events related to Christmas and New Year celebrations are contrary to Islamic culture," explained Sheikh Mohamed Khayrow, director general of the religious affairs ministry, "which could damage the faith of the Muslim community."

In Brunei, nine percent of the population is Christian. Since 2015, publicly celebrating Christmas could bring someone five years in gaol.

The Arab, Asian, and other cultures we're keen to foster in the West are already in the Middle East, Asia, and so forth. Ours aren't, not in any meaningful way. Nor will they be, among people who value themselves. They like their cultures dominating countries.

A Kentucky Fried Chicken restaurant in Beijing isn't multiculturalism. It's a restaurant. We think the whole world's becoming a little bit Western because we see suits in other people's cities, American films in their cinemas, and rich emirs buying our art, but Australian culture never denied us cheap meals in Chinese restaurants or Japanese Godzilla films, from time to time. Other races watch and eat what we produce that they like, if only for the course of a fad. They don't feel the passion for Western cultures we feel for theirs. Nor need they.

Where multiculturalism occurs outside the West, it's nationalistic multiculturalism. Malays, Indonesians, and Egyptians don't enjoy racially homogenous homelands, but they assert their cultures and races. Their countries are Muslim; Allah isn't merely their god, but god. They don't erase their religions, because some of their citizens disagree. They don't defame their heritages or nullify their cultures in empathy with anyone else.

The only one of those countries I've visited is Malaysia. Like other countries outside the West, Malaysia does many things anathemas to us. It denotes an official state religion, Islam, and makes laws of morality. (We make laws of amorality, if not immorality.) It permits and mandates racial and religious discrimination, banning marriage between Muslims and others.

Malays are a race. Their country is Malaysia. In a world of countries, Malaysian culture and people predominate in Malaysia. Yet coming from Western multicultural Australia, I'd never heard of the Hindu festival of lights before seeing Deepavali with my father in Malaysia in 1995. Other Muslim countries, like our supposed allies Kuwait and Bahrain, banned the 2004 film *The Passion of the Christ* for depicting a prophet. Malaysia allowed the sale of tickets through Christian churches. Malaysia's nationalistic multiculturalism acknowledges other people's cultures, while espousing its own.

"*The Islamic world is not multicultural and is not going to be multicultural*," Iranian-born professor of law Afshin Ellian told *Elsevier* magazine in 2016. Migration is economic, and outside the West, migration is within a region; Zimbabweans in South Africa don't give rise to multiculturalism. "*An Afghan worker in Iran remains a second-class citizen who is continuously exposed to humiliation, discrimination and exploitation*," explained Ellian. "*Political and cultural minorities should lead an invisible existence*."

Not in the West. "*New migrants in Europe rapidly learn the rules of multiculturalism – claim your place in society! Minorities do not take the progressive ideals, but the despotism of their country of origin as a starting point.*" There, minorities such as Kurds in Turkey and Syria are harshly oppressed. "*From Morocco to Pakistan or Iran: mass immigration of Europeans are excluded. In most Islamic countries non-Muslims, and especially Europeans, are not allowed to own land, homes, or businesses.*" Ellian warned of a coming era for the West of "*multicultural *backwardness."*

Western multiculturalism is premised upon Western globalism: our rejection of nations. At best, we refuse to allow any culture priority over another; we don't want one offending another. No culture, especially not ours, is preferable to another. No people are expected to predominate, especially not us.

Our countries become cultureless because we're determined cultures not impinge upon each other. When our television stations ceased showing Biblical epic films the night of Good Friday and our governments began allowing cinemas and everything else to open every day of the year, the usual argument for doing so was that the country had become multicultural. Reducing cultures to the least of them leaves none of them worthwhile: cultural nihilism. Our vision of a world without countries becomes a world without cultures.

Other races don't share our vision. Unwinding our cultures from our countries as best as we can, multiculturalism is the framework by which other cultures fill the void left behind.

At worst, Western multiculturalism promotes other cultures at the expense of ours. In September 2016, the United Nations Educational, Scientific and Cultural Organization, UNESCO, and the German government funded eighteen-second television commercials encouraging German women to wear hijabs. "These are the actions of a conquered people," observed American Jewish commentator Pamela Geller.

We've given other races the right to maintain their lifestyles without retaining that right for ourselves. Of all the cultures jostling about, the only ones unvalued are ours. We beg other races not to buy into our cultures and insist our races not remain in, letting their cultures deny us ours until ours have gone. Far from building anything new, we're simply losing the old: cultural genocide. (Eradicating any cultures but ours would be racist.)

In the July 2015 edition of its *Waratah* magazine, the Girl Guides Association of New South Wales and the Australian Capital Territory listed culturally sensitive celebrations and programmes. They were non-denominational songs, non-denominational greetings, and cultural greetings according to ten different Asian cultures, along with National Reconciliation Week and National NAIDOC Week advancing Aborigines and Torres Strait Islanders. Acceptable too were Harmony Day, World Day for Cultural

Diversity, and Refugee Week.

In February 2011, race discrimination commissioner Graeme Innes enthused that the Australian government's National Anti-Racism Partnership and Strategy "affirms that our cultural diversity has defined us over generations." Innes stripped our past as much as our present from our identity, but cultural diversity no more defines one multicultural country than another. It's identity premised upon other people's identities: definition without definition.

Indigenous cultures distinguish colonial European countries from the rest of the multicultural West. We don't care when the indigenous cultures are ours. Europe's indigenous culture is European, so there's nothing to respect. We've only immigrant cultures to celebrate.

The specifics vary a little: British multiculturalism is primarily Indian food, Australian multiculturalism Chinese food, American multiculturalism Mexican food. We prefer multicultural Europe to an Irish Ireland and German Germany, even if we're Irish or German: donor kebabs to Irish stew or apple strudel.

The essence is all much the same: we feast on their foods. What were Western cultures disappear into multicultural monotony. Western multiculturalism becomes no culture, aside from eating and drinking. Only the menus might change.

We're not even looking for the culture that could've been ours. At a time early in the twentieth century that most Americans moved around by nothing better than horse-drawn vehicles, Henry Ford pioneered the mass production of motor vehicles. "If I had asked people what they wanted," he's reputed to have said (although nobody knows when), "they would have said faster horses."

Through the century since then, the West became boring. If anybody asks what we want, the only answer we dare give is more multiculturalism, without thought of our cultures.

Distinctive styles of car became all the same. As my French friend Patrick pointed out, they all look Japanese. We both need to check the logos to know one car from another.

Just as well the rest of the world keeps its countries and cultures. If they'd adopted Western multiculturalism, there'd be sameness and soullessness the world over.

If we have cultures, they're no longer ours. Multiculturalism leaves us overwhelmed by people who believe in themselves and their culture. We assimilate with our immigrants, rather than ask anything of them.

We work like South and East Asians and Jews, but they balance their lives with their cultures, much as we once balanced ours participating in arts, festivals, and the rest of our cultures. When my wife couldn't find tapestry kits in Brussels but only completed tapestries for sale, a storekeeper told her that Belgian women no longer made tapestries. They drove, he said (although so did my wife).

Our forebears rejected gambling as unproductive labour, wasting precious time. We bet like Chinese.

Not only sailors now tattoo themselves like Polynesians. We pierce body parts our forebears kept beautiful.

Instead of societal structures, we have the chaos of Africans, without the tribalism that accords some order in Africa. It's more than the aggressive swearing and expletives unimaginable only a generation or two earlier, or the frivolous way we dress instead of our finery. Following the 2011 presentation night at my eldest daughters' high school, I remarked to the principal about the boys' shirts hanging slovenly over their trousers. We who built empires civilising the world have become a rabble.

English historian David Starkey blamed "black culture" for the English riots of 2011, saying "whites have become black." His comments outraged those few of us who read them. We knew black culture was good. White culture was the problem.

Starkey had a habit of being candid about race. A year later, he defended eight Pakistanis and an Afghan convicted of raping poor English girls in Rochdale. "If you want to look at what happens when you have no sense of common identity, look at Rochdale and events in Rochdale, where you have groups that are absolutely and mutually uncomprehending... Those men were acting within their own cultural norms."

Maintaining any kind of culture is hard when we accommodate everyone else, including the Muslims in Rochdale, without thought of asserting our culture. Starkey placed the lack of dominant cultures at the core of Western countries' problems, although some cultures dominating are worse than none. Our trouble is: we think ours is one of them.

Monocultures needn't be stagnant. They're chances to evolve

upon their people's terms, becoming what they wish to become. An early draft of my manuscript that became *Western Individualism* included the following observation about shopping: "*For as long as principally European women buy perfume and stiletto heel shoes, marketers in European countries won't address too much marketing to Middle Eastern women. They will not address their marketing to men, unless the number of cross-dressing consumers warrants the effort. Still, they'll carefully not alienate those women uncomfortable about sharing their fashions with whisker-faced beefcakes.*"

My Chinese friend Ted convinced me to delete it. Having travelled to oil-rich Middle Eastern emirates, he told me veils didn't deter some women there from wearing the most extravagant of Western clothes, shoes, and styles.

Arab, African, Asian, and Islander societies take what they like and refuse what they don't, while their émigrés in the multicultural West remain defiantly bound to keep what they have. My Greek friend Marie's family immigrated to Australia at a time Southern Europeans were the principal racial minority in Australia. Her mother was keen that Marie honour traditional Greek customs, while the Greeks in Greece left many of them behind.

It's a fascinating irony. We imagine multiculturalism promoting positive change within immigrant communities. Instead, multiculturalism pressures them to hold fast to their cultures. Keeping their affinity to their ancestral lands, traditions, and cultures, they're less likely to evolve than people safe in their homelands. What was supposed to change became changelessness, among immigrants. Cultures evolve among the confidence of monocultural security more than the competitiveness of cruel multiculturalism.

The multicultural West is less of a multicultural world, because Western cultures disappear. It does seem mean-spirited I know, but if there's no Cornish culture in Cornwall, no Western culture in the West, they're not anywhere.

If we believe in a multicultural world, valuing our cultures as we value others, we'll want cultural nationalism too. We'll respect the rights of other races to practice their cultures, while asserting the pre-eminence in our countries not just of indigenous cultures but our cultures too. Other races' cultures prevail in their countries. Our and indigenous cultures would prevail in ours, whatever our faith or without it.

If our countries being Christian seem extraordinary, then notions of a Jewish nation, Hindu nation, Buddhist nations, and abundance of Muslim nations are no more extraordinary. It's not a phobia to enjoy my times in Turkey and Malaysia without wanting to live in a Muslim state, or to enjoy my time in Thailand without wanting to live in a Buddhist state. Wanting to live in a Christian country isn't anti-Semitic, any more than Israel has to be anti-Christian. Armenia, Georgia, East Timor, the Philippines, and several Pacific Islands are Christian countries.

We too could allow our rich cultural traditions a chance to survive and evolve for the better. We could rebuild and build more, without yet knowing what that will be. Our countries might be more religious or more secular, varying over time. They have before now.

8. THE RELIGION OF EUROPE

The West isn't denying Israel its Jewish identity, any Muslim country its Muslim identity, or any other country outside the West its religious identity. Anything other races do to us, they do with our complicity.

Bookshops today offer arrays of books promoting atheism, but little else can compare with American Dan Brown's novels *Angels and Demons* and its sequel *The Da Vinci Code*. I bought the latter when a Macquarie University lecturer Ann-Maree recommended it to me as a murder mystery, before I knew anything about it. The mystery didn't make it one of the biggest selling books of all time. With Brown's opening lie that "*all descriptions of artwork, architecture, documents, and secret rituals in this novel are accurate*," he proceeded to place a fictitious murder in a framework of complete falsification: fiction masquerading as fact, convincing people what is untrue is true.

Accusing the Roman Catholic Church of spending two millennia defrauding the faithful into thinking Christ was the Son of God was a libel no other race would tolerate of its religion. Books preaching anti-Semitism would be burnt. Books libelling Islam would mean the author, publisher, booksellers, and readers would be burnt. Books libelling Buddhism would mean Buddhists burn themselves. (Buddhists are like that.)

Books libelling Christianity sell tens of millions of copies. We make them into films.

Critics in our postmodern West bring dissidents down for one error, but allow adherents to our prevailing ideologies no end of errors. More than enough scholars (including Macquarie University historian Chris Forbes) have demonstrated the nonsense of Brown's writing, but I found the malice so intriguing. We might identify with our religion, but not with our faithful; Brown called himself a Christian without claiming the faith.

We know Christianity to be Western religion. That's why the faithless mock it so freely. Were Christianity not our religion, particularly were we to think of it being another race's religion, then debasing it would be culturally insensitive. It would be racist.

I've never met an atheist who explained his or her atheism as the product of a reasoned investigation into whether God is real. I've only met Christians whose faiths are such a result (along with many for whom it isn't). Nevertheless, in spite of a long history of intelligent Christians, many atheists assume reason is theirs alone. They're also far more interested in publicly challenging Christianity than any other religion.

"*You know it's a myth,*" American Atheists told motorists with a billboard affixed over a New Jersey highway in Christmas 2010, picturing Christ's nativity but no other religion's motif. "*This season, celebrate reason!*"

The Catholic League responded with a billboard on the New York side of the highway. "*You know it's real: this season celebrate Jesus. Merry Christmas from the Catholic League.*"

We don't have debate in the West. We have billboards.

Christianity remains our religious reference point, although white people call upon God less often in prayer than despair. In her first year of high school, my second daughter's sewing class teacher repeatedly complained, "Jesus Christ!" The religion she so tirelessly despoiled may well have been Roman Catholicism. She'd also exclaim, "Bloody Mary!"

She didn't confine herself to blasphemy. In an education system that refused to fail children for fear of harming their delicate self-confidences (but was doubtlessly more concerned about any negative inferences about teachers), she called my daughter and other children, "Idiot!" (Poor teachers call children stupid rather than consider their own shortcomings.) Never again would I presume the sweetness of sewing class teachers.

All over the world there are young people drifting away from the faiths of their forebears, without those of other races mocking their forebears' faiths as white people mock our forebears' faith. When white people loathe their heritage, they loathe Christianity. When they're hostile to the West and all things Western, they're hostile to God.

Among the Old Boys from my school who failed to take up or maintain the faith of our school was Adam Hunt, the younger brother of a friend of mine. His description of the school on his Linked In computer page many decades later was of "*Snotty Private*

Knox Grammar."

Adam was a talented marketer. As part of a campaign in England against racism, Adam developed a poster in which the brains of Europeans, Asians, and Africans were identical, but of racists were puny. It was scientific nonsense, of course, belittling racists as fools, but effective propaganda.

The Foundry advertising agency subsequently appointed Adam as its creative director in Sydney. The television programme *The Gruen Transfer* briefed the agency in 2009 to prepare a television advertisement to "end shape discrimination." The resulting advertisement, filmed in old-fashioned black-and-white, featured four very nasty people smirking as they made the most vicious and humourless of jokes about aborting black people, drowning homosexuals, and incinerating Jews, before a relatively temperate but humourless joke about alcohol and fat women.

Interestingly, the person telling the anti-Semitic joke was Asian, albeit one with an Australian accent. There was not enough interaction between Asians and Jews for either race to be known to ridicule the other, so an Asian telling the joke never seemed credible enough to be provocative. An Arab telling the anti-Semitic joke would have been racist.

The advertisement was so offensive to black people, homosexuals, and Jews, the Australian Broadcasting Corporation wouldn't broadcast it. Instead, the *Anti Prejudice Ad* website broadcast it with a panel discussion about it, providing a fascinating insight into how very skilled people have set about changing Western thinking.

"I hated every single person in that ad," said panel host Wil Anderson.

"My point," explained Adam, "was to say that if you discriminate against somebody on the basis of their shape, you're no different from those other sorts of discrimination."

The panellists equated jokes with discrimination and hating people, unconcerned whether a person the subject of a joke ever heard it. They presumed discrimination was moronic and mean, without deliberation upon the reasons people discriminate. There was no consideration of reasoned argument, presumably because they believed there couldn't be any with what one panellist called "bigoted idiots." I was left suspecting there could no longer be reasoned argument with anyone.

Another panellist, Todd Samson I think, distinguished Anderson from racists by saying Anderson was "sensitive." He wasn't sensitive to people who discriminate.

"For me, discrimination is the most offensive thing," said Adam. "Discrimination is ugly, and if you want somebody to stop doing something you've got to show them how ugly it is… Changing the brand of beer that somebody drinks is actually not as difficult as changing the way someone thinks."

Campaigns mould our minds. For all the rights we boast in our supposedly free societies, our right isn't to think as we choose but as we're taught to think.

At the end of the discussion, Anderson asked, "If someone can make me a list of people I can actually still make fun of…"

"The white Australian male," responded Samson, although he presumably meant only heterosexual ones. They all laughed, those white Australian males. "You can go to town!"

"I mean Amish people," said Anderson. "They're not watching." White people would feel offence at any slight upon other races and rush to complain whether or not they were watching, but would enjoy jokes against the puritanical white Christian Amish.

For all Adam's proselytization about discrimination being ugly, a year earlier, his design company Goatboy (also known as Goat Boy) sold tee shirts bearing slogans that police were "*targeting fat chicks.*" Adam didn't think misogyny was ugly.

Eva Cox from the Women's Electoral Lobby condemned those designs. She called them "tasteless, crappy, crass, and stupid."

As Adam repeatedly said, his material was very clever and ironic. The furore taught him not to produce shirts against women anymore.

Adam's journey of personal discovery hadn't gone very far. His 'Goatboy loves Women' range retained a shirt modelled on the posters for the film *Jaws*. A recent shark attack on Bondi Beach inconveniently involved a man, but Adam's design headed "*Bondi*" was of a shark preparing to eat a white woman, as had the film posters. Adam was, or became, romantically involved with a Taiwanese woman.

Nor did Adam think discrimination against Roman Catholics was ugly. His particular passion was the Roman Catholic Church's World Youth Day in Sydney, 2008. "*Sponsor a lion for World Youth*

Day," said one slogan Goatboy offered, contemplating a slaughter. "*300,000 Catholics in one stadium*."

Newspaper columnist Elizabeth Farrelly didn't distinguish between denominations when, in 2011, she described the Christians in her high school class when she was fifteen years old as "*Jesus freakery*." She refused to consider any relationship between crime and race or between crime and coming from fatherless families, in spite of the evidence otherwise, but wrote that "*the church is demonstrably rife with paedophilia*."

She blamed the London riots that year and threats to civilisation not on immigration but on Christianity. "*And it's this presumption of divine access in order to enforce uniformity – this sense of entitlement – that is the real link to the London rioters, and the real threat to civilised life, depending as it does on the wilful abandonment of reason and merit for the hate-filled, know-nothing demagoguery of the mob.*"

The mob to which Farrelly referred weren't the rioters who'd burnt and destroyed parts of London, but Christians wanting to keep marriage heterosexual. None of those Christians rioted so far as I was aware. Nor do I imagine them having spurred the rioters to their crimes. Farrelly seems to have been unmarried.

Western multiculturalism is never more virulent than when set upon Christianity. While welcoming the religions of other races, we strive to bring our religion down.

In such an atmosphere, little wonder that the *Daily Telegraph* newspaper made no mention of eight people involved in a brawl in the Parramatta business district in July 2012, in which Patrick Crowe was stabbed with a knife and died, being Islanders. Instead, it made much of a fifteen-year-old girl facing possible murder charges being a "*regular singer in her church community choir.*" That was doubtlessly an Islander church choir.

Anti-Semitism means prejudice against Jews by their race or religion, no matter how minor. There's no corresponding word for prejudice against Christians, no matter how rabid.

Much as we've done with race, we've stopped mentioning the religions of wrongdoers who aren't Christian. We might speak instead of their religious background, especially as regards Muslims. It makes religion their history, although it denies them the element of choice. If people choose their religion, then it's not really background, except to the story. Religion becomes a minor descriptor, a matter of incidental fact, but a descriptor and fact nevertheless.

Similarly, we sometimes speak of a Muslim's religious orientation. It's the language we use to make homosexuality appear intrinsic to a person and so discrimination against homosexuals unjust, although Muslims continue to condemn homosexuality. (We don't condemn much, except white Christian discrimination.) I can't imagine suicide bombers going to their deaths merely as people of an Islamic background.

If we're not blaming religion in general for war and holocaust, then our religion is to blame. In 2011, on a Sunday of all days, under the heading 'Church and hate,' journalist Peter FitzSimons asked, "*can serious Christians explain why God bothered to create Muslims if their beliefs are an abomination to him and Vicky-Versa?*" FitzSimons liked Muslims, possibly because Muslims disliked Christians, but if religion is a matter of birth, not choice, then FitzSimons was a Christian, although not a serious one. Heterosexual as he was, he defended homosexuality on the basis "*your God*" created homosexuals too.

If we make gods of other people, then they would probably agree, but if other races have their religious backgrounds and orientations, then we do too. To be descended of ancient European peoples is to have a Christian orientation, at least for the last millennium or two, unless we think our Western capacity for choice overcomes it (as we no longer imagine choice of homosexuality). What we happen to believe can hardly change an orientation. We're still what we were in 1914, Christian European, however much we're trying not to be. We can't escape our religion by birth.

The West is trying hard to reorient. "*I'm a non-believer, loud and proud,*" headed one of FitzSimons Sunday columns in 2010, employing the language of homosexual defiance. "*I proclaim, I boast, I rejoice in, I 'bang on endlessly, until everyone gets a nose bleed, and wishes I would shut up...' etc, about being an atheist.*"

Peter had come a long way from Knox Grammar School, where he was in the year ahead of me. In 2016, Peter and I sat beside each other at the funeral of our past teacher, Alan Marsden.

Thirty-three years after I finished my schooling, a bagpiper ushered more than a hundred of us to a President's Dinner for the Old Knox Grammarians Association. Old paintings hung from the walls of the Killara Golf Club; they and the clubhouse were no less beautiful because I wasn't a member. Listening to the personable speeches, I realised my affection for the school I'd attended for eleven years wasn't a judgement on the school of brown brick walls. It reflected the school having been mine: my heritage.

Having been so poor a student of the bagpipes now matters less to me than having been a student of them at all. I played cricket poorly, but enjoyably.

Four years later, the President's Dinner was at the school. I realised that when we as races feel what the old boys and their wives felt that night as a school, we'll be nations again.

Knox didn't make me Presbyterian, but Presbyterianism is part of my culture, enmeshed with everything Scottish. So are Anglicanism and Roman Catholicism, enmeshed with everything British and European.

Perceptions of God affect people's thoughts and feelings about everything. So do race, family, gender, and experiences. We don't choose our race (which is much of the reason we don't like race anymore), but our ancestors choosing Christianity means we're born to the faith, just as other races are born to theirs. Individuals might renounce their faith and even loathe themselves for having held it, but European peoples are Christian. Ours may be the fading cloud of Christendom, but no European or distant child of Europe can speak from any other place. We don't love other cultures by dismissing our own.

9. PERSPECTIVES

Most peoples' views of the world can't help but be from their perspectives. Indians have an Indian-centric view, Nepalese a Nepalese-centric view. A people's perspective is more than two eyes alone ever see.

"When I grew up," said Anne Foley, principal of Kennedy School in Somerville, Massachusetts in 2011, "I was taught from a very European perspective of history, and it was both embarrassing and enlightening to me when I learned other perspectives." She'd responded to the multitude of races in her district by adopting Native American and Caribbean perspectives of explorer Christopher Columbus, witchcraft, and everything else. "I want our children and families to know that we are aware of those other perspectives."

About the only perspectives of which Western children and families are unaware are their own. Foley banned from the school Columbus Day and Halloween, because they were European (however lost Halloween's origins are in pumpkins and ghosts). She considered banning Thanksgiving.

Western peoples dismiss our particular perspectives as if we can ever really have another, but individualism, multiculturalism, and diversity are our new Western perspectives. Race remains at the forefront of our thinking, but they're the races of everyone else. We hear other people's histories, cloaked in our deprecation. Our view is no less Eurocentric for being our contempt for our forebears. We rarely look back to discover how recently we changed.

The author of books about Queen Elizabeth I and the private life of King Henry VIII, historian David Starkey in 2012 called for a "genuine approach to the teaching of English history," describing our past as it was and not as we and others malign it to be. "It is a fundamental story, and it seems to me that if we are to make this highly diverse society work, and I desperately hope that we do, what we should be focusing on is the astonishing record of change without revolution in English history in which the political system of king, lords and commoners, has proved flexible enough to spread from a tiny, deeply selective electorate to a wider and wider group who have been incorporated, have been brought in and made to feel welcome." He believed that could create a common identity, overcoming multiculturalism.

Parliamentarian Malcolm Turnbull explicitly rejected complexion, religion, and ethnicity as measures of being Australian in 2011. "We are defined as Australians because of the commitment to the shared political values of this country," he said, politics being so important to us. It was an ideological sense of nationhood, without race or culture. "That's why our society is so inclusive."

We're selectively inclusive. In a delightful half-truth, Turnbull said putting down any religion, culture, or race was "unhelpful" in the integration of people from around the world, but promoting republicanism and the end of constitutional monarchy in Australia, he'd happily put down his race: the British.

When I was young, I'd wanted Australia to become a republic for many reasons, including my naïve belief republics were more democratic and reflective of a popular will than monarchies, but there was nothing democratic about the republic proposed in the 1999 Australian referendum. An Australian president appointed by parliament would replace an Australian governor-general appointed by the Queen. The new head of state would be no more popularly elected than the old.

The campaign for an Australian republic was unconcerned with democracy. It was predicated upon the rejection of our sovereign being British, complaining about any trace of accession to Britain as we would never complain of acceding to the United Nations or any country in Asia. People who normally decry nationalism for being narrow-minded bigotry and racist xenophobia claim the nationalist mantle to demand the end of the British monarchy in Australia. A British monarch, they argue, offers nothing to Australians who aren't of British ancestry.

I could accept other races saying as much, but not Australian British. I campaigned against the 1999 republic, while rumour was that Turnbull intended to become Australia's first president.

At least Turnbull liked the Roman Catholic tradition. He'd converted to his wife's faith having been, in some measure, a

Presbyterian. He nevertheless rejected the Roman Catholic Church's teaching with which he disagreed.

In his last year of primary school, my second son's teacher told the class the British invaded Australia in 1788. He rejected my son saying we wouldn't be here, but for the British. The teacher also insisted the British never invented anything. After I pointed out to my son the steam engine, without proceeding to list British inventions that would have taken me days or weeks to name, I remarked upon the teacher's self-loathing. He was British.

The teacher had converted to Judaism. Increasingly since the Second World War, Jewish perspectives of our forebears and us have become ours, looking back through the thick prism of Holocaust.

Other races aren't as submissive as we are. The last Thursday of the winter school term, in her first year of high school, my eldest daughter was again among the students at a two-day arts workshop. Driving home early that evening, she mentioned my eldest son's Persian friend David calling her Jewish for attending a high school significantly populated by Jews. He mocked her becoming "Jewisher."

As we neared our home, my daughter lambasted the primary school we passed, at which she'd finished being a pupil nine months earlier. "We didn't learn anything," she complained, "because we were so busy learning Australia's culture is having many cultures."

Indeed it is: Persian, Jewish, Vietnamese... The only culture it's not is Australian, at least not European Australian. We strive to undo our past cultural colonisation, while our immigrants' cultural imperialism delights us.

Trying hard to make multiculturalism work, we teach our children about everyone else (the good bits anyway). Premier Barry O'Farrell in 2011 was keen to increase the foisting of Asian cultures and languages on a New South Wales school system that already left children with little knowledge of European cultures and language.

While discussing the problems of multiculturalism would be racist, we have no qualms about calling the remnants of our racial homogeneity a problem. "There are incredibly vibrant parts of this city," said O'Farrell of Sydney, "and I suspect there are still other parts of this city that are very monocultural."

Parts of the city racially homogenous with other races we call multicultural. They're vibrant for no other reason than the people not being us. O'Farrell was preparing for a trip to Asia to attract more immigrants.

The American Department of Education had identified Arabic as a "language of the future." It thus approved funding through its Foreign Language Assistance Programme for the teaching of not just the Arabic language, but also Arab culture, government, art, traditions, and history (doubtlessly a far more generous treatment, being from an Arab perspective, than we teach of ours).

Early in 2011, the Mansfield Independent School District in Texas proposed the studies be mandatory at Cross Timbers Intermediate School and Kenneth Davis Elementary School and optional at the T.A. Howard Middle School and Summit High School. Superintendent Bob Morrison stressed the studies excluded religion, as if culture could.

Born in the Middle East but raised in America, Kheirieh Hannun wanted her son and others like him to learn more about their culture. That wasn't American. It was Arab.

We're not so interested in our children learning about our cultures, art, traditions, and history. "We need to think globally and act locally," said Trisha Savage in support of the Mansfield proposal, repeating one of our most ubiquitous slogans without thought as to what it might mean. It could mean her children learning about their cultural heritage, much as the Arabs were keen to learn theirs. (We used to think locally and act globally, but that was imperialism.)

Not all Mansfield parents were immediately eager for their children to learn so much about Arabs, although that might've been because they'd not been consulted. The day the school district announced the plan, it deferred implementation while parents were consulted. (We can do all sorts of terrible things, provided we consult.)

"*The curriculum is where a particular story of the world is set up, either deliberately or inadvertently,*" wrote Lyn Yates, an editor of the *Routledge Yearbook 2011: Curriculum in Today's World*. "*Schools show what is valued both by the subjects they make compulsory and the processes they emphasise, and also by what they teach directly.*"

Pakistani textbooks and religious madrasa schools nurtured sentiments against India and the West. (Western textbooks and schools did the same, but not against India.)

"*Other countries,*" wrote Yates, "*have been using curriculum change to try to modify and even de-emphasise national identities compared with outwardly facing ones.*" Brazil was trying to instil a new national image around multiculturalism. (It made Brazil very Western.)

The postmodern West is very different to the rest of the world. It always is. No countries face outward more than those of East Asia, most strikingly China, Japan, and South Korea, but they remain emphatic about their national identities. Only we think facing outward requires erasing our national identities. Western countries face outwards, but not towards our peoples.

No wonder Western education systems lag behind those in Asia. While our school curricula focus on equality and other races, East Asians focus upon excellence and their national interests. "*China has moved to make science, mathematics and competitive achievement the prominent agenda...,*" wrote Yates.

Through ten years from 1966, the Cultural Revolution traumatically set about eradicating Chinese traditions and culture (along with capitalism) in favour of communism. Following Chairman Mao Zedong's death in 1976, Chinese governments slowly revived traditional Chinese beliefs, including Buddhism and Taoism. "Sensitive topics are banned," said Feng Chongyi of the China Research Centre at the University of Technology, Sydney in 2012. "So there's been a revival of popular religion...state television and films all reinforce that concept of *Long Zi Long Sun.*" Chinese associate dragon son, dragon grandson with good luck, power, and wealth. "There has also been a rise of nationalism, with an emphasis on Confucianism and China's national symbols."

Western governments also ban sensitive topics, although different topics to those banned in China. Our television and films aren't reviving our religion or nationalism, but we're still amidst our cultural revolution.

In Australia, an Australian perspective would've been insular and a European perspective racist. Established in 2008, the National Curriculum Board directed that subjects be taught from an Asian perspective. (We'd decided Australia is part of Asia, but Papua New Guinea is closer than Australia to Asia without imagining itself Asian.) Australia's engagement with Asia was one of three multidiscipline priorities intended to pervade the curriculum. Australia's engagement with the rest of the West and our heritage never rated a mention.

Following that directive, the Australian Curriculum Studies Association and University of Melbourne's Centre for Excellence in Islamic Studies sponsored workshops free to teachers in 2010 to overcome a *"degree of prejudice and ignorance about Islam and Muslims."* (Linking prejudice with ignorance rather than knowledge is all very Western, but knowledge had created the prejudice.) The workshops blamed people's poor opinions of Muslims on the media. (Journalists rarely so much as hinted at the religion of Muslim criminals, terrorists, and other wrongdoers, but people knew anyway.)

Authors of the booklet *Learning from One Another: Bringing Muslim Perspectives into Australian Schools* complained that *"most texts used in Australian English classes still have a Western or European perspective."* They wanted English taught from a Muslim perspective.

They also wanted the same of science and history, complaining that *"students with a Euro-centric version of history denies them the opportunity to evaluate different perspectives on past world events."* (Certainly, our new Western perspective leaves little scope for considering our forebears weren't horrible.) *"Students will come to appreciate that there are many valid worldviews and perspectives."* (We've dismissed our forebears' world views and perspectives for being invalid.)

Stating that Islam grew throughout the Mediterranean and parts of Europe because *"many peoples of the newly conquered regions converted to Islam,"* ignored the compulsion upon those conquered peoples, often upon threat of death. *"Those who did not were allowed to live peacefully and practice their faith as long as they abided by the law of the land,"* omitted to mention that Islamic law imposed upon Christians and Jews the subordinate status of dhimmi. Our legal and social rights were inferior to those of Muslims. We paid special taxes.

Still, I respect Muslims presenting their best impressions, even of their invasions. We present our worst impressions, along with the best of everyone else. We think it's polite.

Also pervading Australia's national curriculum were Aboriginal issues and sustainability. The government in 2010 proposed a curriculum requiring high school children to learn about Aboriginal culture, families, and social structure.

My wife, her parents, and I attended the annual awards ceremony at my eldest son's high school in his penultimate year, because he'd won the modern history prize. In his address, the school principal spoke at length about the school's relationship with a country school populated primarily with Aborigines. Most fascinating was the principal's endorsement of what he considered a broad education, but the culture he wanted students to learn wasn't their own. "The day a year-seven or a year-nine student chooses Aboriginal studies instead of mathematics or science because he wants to," he told his audience, "will be a cause of great optimism."

Clearly, students were choosing Aboriginal studies without wanting to. I preferred my children learn mathematics and science. The culture I want them to learn is ours.

Between the indigenous and the immigrant was our European history and heritage in which we're less interested, unless it's political or economic. The Australian Curriculum Assessment and Reporting Authority issued a national curriculum that contained a course, 'The Development of Australian Identity,' including the history of the trade union movement and formation of the Labor Party. Once in a while, the children can put aside hearing how awful we were.

In May 2010, the Texas curriculum board adopted a social studies curriculum increasing the emphasis on Biblical influences on American history, reducing the emphasis on slavery and civil rights, and criticising overseas aid programmes. Only in the West is a patriotic curriculum controversial.

Any education system is woefully incomplete if it doesn't teach children their culture and history. There might be value in knowing something of other cultures because there might be value in better understanding other races, but that depends upon us knowing ours beforehand. The more we learn of other races in our finite lives on earth, the less we learn of ourselves. We don't know anything at all.

When I was a child, Russians seemed to have forgotten Mother Russia: the title of a book on my bedroom shelves. Russia began her experiment with ideology sooner than we did: after the First World War rather than the Second. She began recovering her self-belief sooner than we have.

The collapse of the Soviet Union in 1991 led to a Russian curriculum initially emphasising what a governing elite considered common human values (as we do in the West), before regaining something of her soul by restoring national and patriotic themes. Almost a century after the Russian Revolution, Russia rediscovered

Mother Russia. She rediscovered Europe.

While resisting the nationalism that would've returned to Russians and other races within the Russian Federation their countries, Prime Minister Vladimir Putin (between his terms as president) sounded positively nationalistic aside Western Europe, the Americas, and Australasia in 2012. *"The Russian people,"* he wrote, *"the Russian culture is the glue holding together the unique fabric of this civilisation."* Russian language and culture dominated, while other races enjoyed rights to theirs.

By April 2014, Russia's determination to protect her people and civilisation led the government to develop a culture policy premised upon the notion that "Russia is not Europe." Twenty-five professors from the Russian Academy of Sciences wrote an open letter rejecting that interpretation of Russian history. What struck me wasn't that Russia is European, but that much of Europe and the rest of the West no longer are.

10. CULTURELESS INDIVIDUALISM

In 1607, venture capitalists of the Virginia Company established the Jamestown colony. It remained the capital of the Virginia colony for ninety-two years. Like the ideals Jefferson espoused in his Declaration of Independence, business served civilisation. Witnessing the Great War, America began losing her sense of being European civilisation. Business and ideals remained.

"The chief business of the American people is business," said President Calvin Coolidge in a speech titled 'The Press under a Free Government' delivered to the American Society of Newspaper Editors on the seventeenth of January 1925. "The chief ideal of the American people is idealism." A century later, the West's *only* business is business, our *only* ideals our ideologies.

Our standards and attitudes weren't other peoples. They didn't contribute to us forming them.

In the third round of the 2013 American Masters golf tournament in Augusta, black American Tiger Woods illegally dropped his ball on the fifteenth hole. Furthermore, he overlooked his two-stroke penalty when handing in his incorrect score card. Golfers like Nick Faldo called for Woods to resign as they would have resigned, but Woods refused. What struck me through it all wasn't the determination of journalists like Michael Rosenberg to defend Woods, but our presumption that etiquette is universal.

Golf was slower than other sports to give up its niceties, presumably because it remained European. Competition as much as multiculturalism commands young white people give up our niceties too.

According to a speaker at an Australian Corporate Lawyers' Association conference early in the 1990s, Hong Kong people pressed the buttons to close the doors immediately upon stepping into lifts. They didn't want other passengers delaying their journeys.

In 2007, a speaker to an association lunch said Vietnamese normally interrupted meetings to take telephone calls. I've only seen the practice in Australia at a fund management company, employing more East Asians than any other company for which I've worked.

Business is frenetic through parts of Asia as it wasn't in the West; the Chinese were more frenetic than the more relaxed Malays when I visited Malaysia. Thais could be busy or not when I was in Thailand, but there were few Chinese with whom I could compare them. Races frenetic in one country don't relax in another, not completely anyway.

They might have their etiquette among their own in other contexts. We don't. For all our talk of being tolerant, we grow tired of being courteous to people who aren't courteous to us. The more we've become surrounded by rude people, the ruder we've become. We don't notice, because we forget how we used to be. If we don't forget, we deride. Without social etiquette, we've lost business etiquette.

I don't think anyone more completely personified our Western rejection of religion than Kim. Amidst a weekly mining industry lunch at the Spicy Island restaurant, North Sydney, long before we worked together, I joked about people rising from the dead every two thousand years or so. "Not even then," said Kim, more serious than he needed to be. For all that white people complain about Christians espousing faith, I've never heard any espouse faith outside church as often as some atheists espouse atheism.

My first Christmas working at Golden Cross Resources Limited, the Christmas party, of sorts, in 2008 was a small barbecue at Kim's home with no mention of Christmas. (Employees don't expect to be invited to directors' homes, or even being shown photographs, so that was rather nice.) Kim generously gave the few company employees bottles of McLaren Vale red wine, but after spending Christmas Eve morning away from the office shopping, he complained about Christmas Day and Boxing Day interrupting work.

"It hasn't interrupted me," I replied. The day was Wednesday. I'd worked Monday and Tuesday. Being as new as I was to the role employing me three days a week, my priority was marketing myself. Whatever three days I worked of a week, public holidays were among the other two days.

The theme of his words was picked up by a message he sent to another chief executive about proposals for amending an agreement between the two companies. "…*hope to get back to you fairly soon,*" wrote Kim, "*the next few days being interrupted by some sort of traditional holiday...*"

I wished him a "Merry Christmas," as I wished everyone with whom I spoke and some of the people to whom I sent messages that day. As kind as he was with his best wishes back to me, Kim wouldn't mention Christmas; heaven forbid. His wasn't some sensitivity less I be something other than Christian, but a complete refusal to touch Christian story.

Dave Timms was the only other director with whom I worked who gave Christmas presents to employees. He gave bottles of wine, with Christmas ribbons around the neck, for the few people at the office on Christmas Eve.

Perhaps something mellowed Kim a little. Perhaps Dave (the founder of the company) inspired him a little, as only directors can inspire each other. Kim's last electronic message that day, at least to other directors and me, wished that we all "*Have good Xmas & New Year.*"

For a year or two thereafter, if the office manageress was in the mood, a few decorations of tinsel and trimmings adorned the offices; there could be more tinsel than employees. Dave gave us presents each year, but there were no more company parties. Four years after I arrived, there was nothing. The only mention of Christmas activity was my wry observation to Kim that the company was saving money by not hosting Christmas lunches anymore. I was the only employee to wish anyone a Merry Christmas. The only person giving gifts was a young Chinese woman, Amy, who gave each of us chocolates.

Early in 2010, at a rare staff lunch at the Blue Gum Hotel to which I was invited, Kim again mentioned Christianity. The more he spoke, the more I realised that his antagonism to his British heritage and his antagonism to Christianity were the same antagonism, in spite of him having said, as the West says, "all religions are the same."

"I know lots of atheists," I said, "but..."

"They're all nice, are they?" he interrupted.

"You're the only one who's evangelical about it."

"This Peter Jensen and George Pell," he said, of the Anglican and Roman Catholic archbishops of Sydney. "They want to control people."

"I don't see that," I told him. "They don't control me or anyone

I know."

The control close to our hearts is upon us. Most of my time, I could do what I liked, as long as I performed my chores quickly, didn't spend money, and didn't get in Kim's way. He was the first manager who forbade me from obtaining expert advice without his prior approval, after the first time I did. It can only have hurt that the advice was that we couldn't immediately issue the rights offer document I'd drafted (although a company like ours had issued a similar one). The hindrances irritating us can be the most minor of rules by which a society, including a commercial society, function.

In the face of our individualism, religion isn't a matter of fact, faith, or identity. It's an imposition.

"You just keep putting up hurdles," Kim told me angrily, with people walking past and around us after a Sydney Mining Club lunch at the Tattersalls Club, the first Thursday of March 2010. (He'd been a corporate guest, and we'd sat at different tables during the meal.) The most recent hurdle was the stock exchange rules mandating the timetables by which companies could raise money by rights issues, set by reference to business days. The completion of the process would be deferred by two days for the Easter public holidays, so Kim's anger quickly extended to all "you religious types!"

"Blame the Romans," I responded. "They crucified Him."

Blaming the Jews would've been anti-Semitism. We'd become used to blaming Europeans for everything.

The first working day after the Easter break 2010, I was in Kim's office for a matter of work, but work wasn't his first thought. "Before we talk about that," he said angrily, "why can't you God-botherers let me buy a beer on Friday? I was in a pub and they could sell me beer to drink, but not to take away with me. It's an imposition on my liberties!"

"When I was in Malaysia," I told him, "on the east coast of the peninsular, I couldn't buy alcohol at all. It wasn't a big deal."

"You Christians, you're almost as bad as the Muslims."

There didn't seem to be any point in arguing, as I leant against the bookcase on which stood Kim's geology books and Chinese ornaments. Kim wasn't demanding rights as profound as those set forth in Magna Carta or the American Declaration of Independence. His demands weren't those that inspired revolutionaries in France in 1789. He just wanted to buy beer on

Good Friday from a pub in the country, and take it away with him.

Western individual rights don't come from God, but from a rejection of God: a rejection of every restriction upon a person doing whatever he or she wants to do, immediately. What so infuriated Kim was any semblance of a sense that religion could, in any indirect, incidental, or most trivial of ways for the briefest of moments, diminish his complete individual liberty. Drinking beer in a pub, as I couldn't have done on the east coast of the Malaysian peninsular, wasn't enough. Atheism is individualism.

When Kim complained about holidays interrupting the working year, at a meeting with the company auditors the second Thursday of March 2010, he didn't just complain about Christmas, Easter, and the Western New Year. In the list he rattled away, he included the holiday that most comprehensively caused people, Chinese people anyway, to stop working for longest: Chinese New Year.

I reminded him of those words two days before Good Friday when, back in his office, Kim again complained about the intrusion of Easter. "You told us," I said, "although to your credit, you didn't complain just about religious holidays. There was New Year, Chinese New Year, Australia Day, Anzac Day..." (He'd not mentioned Australia's national day and the Australia and New Zealand day for remembering fallen soldiers, but that was the spirit of what he'd said.)

"There shouldn't be any public holidays," Kim confirmed. They interrupted business, if only for a day. Before I could dwell too much on a life wholly of work, he explained. "You should have your own holidays." I'd already picked up from the printer his bookings for a hotel that coming short week in Adelaide, although I didn't know if that was for work or holiday. "It should be like me, when I was a young geologist. When we used to work, we'd work six days a week, have one day off. You could do what you like, catch up on some work, drawings..."

"Go to church?"

"Then after five weeks, go somewhere for a whole week. We'd have to pay for everything, but we'd have those weekends off, so it would be nine days, from Friday to Monday, and we could do what we wanted."

His was a perfectly individualistic vision, with no sense of society. There'd be no common holidays, festivals, or anything for people to share. Premised upon our postmodern individualism, we have no national cultures because we have no nations.

We're not cultures. We're economies.

We're not citizens. We're employees.

Lives estranged from religion lose more than our religious culture. They leave the rest of our cultures behind. It's no coincidence that the postmodern West operates without religion and has no culture, not in any meaningful way. We're culturally empty.

Other races don't reduce their lives to commercial transactions as we do. Warwick, a lawyer then active in our family's Uniting church, believed Japan has so many public holidays *because* they interrupt economic activity. It wants its people to think about things other than business. Japan is a country, society, and culture, as we no longer are.

We without nations have nothing national, no national anything, no ways of life. Other people's lifestyles aren't ours to notice, unless we feel they affect us. We have no interest in lifestyles past generations experienced. When we were a people possessing a culture, the religious and irreligious possessed our festivals, but we individuals feel no greater ownership of the traditions our religions bequeathed us than the rest of our cultural heritage. We have no traditions beyond those we individuals each make for ourselves, one year to the next, one week to the next.

Kim's atheism didn't prevent him from including in his reply to the chairman at a board meeting, the second day of September 2011, "for Christ's sake." His atheism might even have inspired it, although the discussion was less about an immortal deity than about coal tenements in Queensland.

A year later, after I advised Kim to defer an unimportant stock exchange announcement to Monday morning so people might see it, he told me to "F*** off!" People not willing to hear chief executives swear at them, even when helping them, shouldn't be lawyers.

Our postmodern festivals are those like the coloured lights on city buildings of the annual Vivid festivals in Sydney I first saw in 2013. We can see them in our time whatever moment of night we choose, alone in the dark or with friends. We can see them with a scout or church group, by which my youngest son and eldest daughter respectively saw Vivid in 2015. We can see them as a family, although the hours we expended one wet winter Saturday night in 2013 for my children bar one to see the *Doctor Who* spectacle on the Customs House building wasn't worth it. The five-minute show was no more than a television trailer could be.

Like the coloured lights across the Perth Council House I saw in 2010, our pretty postmodern festivals come without history or cultural context. The whole world can enjoy them without feeling any one people own them: our best efforts towards a post-racial, multicultural culture. They come without public holidays, so nobody misses a chance to work, study, or shop if they choose not to participate. They also come without story, meaning, or substance. Facile and forgettable, I couldn't be bothered seeing anything of the Vivid festivals again, unless I'm nearby anyway.

All cultures are racist. Without race, there's no commonality. Individuals estranged from each other can never amount to a culture. There's only economics and ideology, as the West became. For us to salvage our societies and civilisation, we need to feel we're a people.

11. OWNING CULTURE

Without collective identities, we have no architectural styles, beyond the particular homes and apartments we own. If we rent, we don't even have that.

When we ceased being a people, we ceased possessing our culture and heritage. We have no music, literature, painting, or sculpture, beyond what we each craft ourselves. Few of us do. We might produce it for pleasure or profit for sale to other individuals, if art's our profession.

Those of us unable to compose or craft have no arts, beyond those we buy. We own a canvas hanging from our wall, and books and discs we've not discarded. We might appreciate upon what we muse in a gallery and enjoy what we hear from a radio, but never consider it ours. Perhaps the artist feels a small sense of original enterprise, or perhaps the sale being complete her senses move along. For the rest of us, it's not our creation. We're not a people to possess it.

We've stopped treating arts and learning as being those of our people concerned in creating our culture. They're of individuals acting alone. We don't wonder whether anyone but Europeans could produce a magical boy wizard or any of a thousand other memorable characters. There's only our blithe assumption that anything good we can do, everyone else can do too. What might've been cause for pride no longer is.

We no longer speak proudly of our people's achievements, although I imagine those of us doing so being shouted down for their narrowness and bigotry. No other race produced our science, technology, or fine arts, but when we appreciate them, it's not for being ours. They disappear into a sense of being human achievements, for which the whole world shares equally. Our good culture, we call everyone's (although our failings are ours alone). A naked peasant boy scaling the trunk of a palm tree in the Solomon Islands has as much right to feel pride for the writings of Goethe and Schiller as would a German in a Düsseldorf library.

The island boy feels no pride. Neither does the German.

We've been doing that for a while. "That's one small step for a man," said American astronaut Neil Armstrong landing on the moon in 1969, "one giant leap for mankind."

He and his fellow American Buzz Aldrin didn't see their achievement as one for Americans or European peoples, but for all people. "*Here men from the planet Earth first set foot upon the Moon,*" said the plaque they left behind, along with a mission patch and medals commemorating American and Russian space explorers who'd died trying to breach Earth's atmospheric curtain. "*July 1969 A.D. We came in peace for all mankind.*"

We share our successes with humanity. "I think we're going to the moon because it's in the nature of the human being to face challenges," Armstrong told a press conference for the Apollo moon missions. "It's by the nature of his deep inner soul... We're required to do these things, just as salmon swim upstream."

Taking upon challenges was never a human being's nature, not without reason. It was European nature. Standing in Washington's Smithsonian Museum (which I visited at Mike's suggestion one Saturday afternoon, before meeting him for dinner in 1998), the Apollo landing craft remained impressive for its technology, but most of all its adventure. It was America bold and optimistic, as she'd rarely been of late.

By 2010, the central missions of the North American Space Administration were no longer landing Americans on the moon. Rather than anything scientific or technological, the missions were political.

"When I became the NASA administrator," said Charles Bolden, "or before I became the NASA administrator," President Barack Obama "charged me with three things. One was he wanted me to help re-inspire children to want to get into science and math, he wanted me to expand our international relationships, and third, and perhaps foremost, he wanted me to find a way to reach out to the Muslim world and engage much more with dominantly Muslim nations to help them feel good about their historic contribution to science...and math and engineering."

Muslims already felt good about their historic contributions to science, mathematics, engineering, and everything else: more than we feel about ours. A young American Arab had made a short film I'd seen boasting of Arab accomplishments in mathematics, as no white American dared for his or her race.

Races but ours don't trivialise their people's triumphs, reducing them to those of mankind. Their achievements are theirs. The old Beijing observatory I visited in 1988 spoke proudly of Chinese astronomy and learning, as no Western historical site I've visited claimed collective credit by race.

With collective identities, they enjoy cultural identities. They own their cultures: their people's paintings beyond any affixed to their walls, literature beyond any books on their shelves, and music beyond any discs that they play. They have their pride and fervour. They also have ours.

Rob, a merchant banker and director of Holyman Limited, was one of several investors in an Aboriginal art gallery in Sydney during the 1990s. With white people so keen on other races' art and so many tourists coming to Sydney, I assumed the gallery would succeed. It didn't. Aborigines and we alike didn't want us profiting from Aboriginal art.

We defer to other people's cultures, because those cultures are theirs. Welsh writers as much as Bangladeshi meat cutters can write Welsh novels, but only Bangladeshis can write Bangladeshi novels, if there are any.

We can't have what isn't ours. Critics accused American singer Katy Perry of cultural appropriation after she performed her song 'Unconditionally' with a Japanese theme at the 2013 American Music Awards. *"This is the performance equivalent of an offensive Halloween costume,"* wrote one irate person on the Twitter website.

When fashion writer Alyx Gorman compiled her list of the ten worst trends in fashion in 2011, the worst wasn't anything to do with hemlines, colour, or even fashion, let alone lifeless-looking models with dehumanised faces. It was racism, not in designs but expressed by designers.

Racism matters more to us than everything else, except race. Prague held a Black Fashion Week in 2011, as did Montreal in 2012. In Paris' Black Fashion Week, about fifteen black designers from Africa and living in France, Haiti, and America presented their collections at the chic *Pavillon Cambon Capucines*.

Yet, Australian fashion journalist Clem Bastow objected when the New York Fashion Week collections for 2012 and 2013 included Aboriginal art. *"I don't think the issue of institutional racism and discrimination can be completely divorced from the question of cultural appropriation. They feed into one another… Reducing an entire culture to a simple 'inspiration' for your outfit, art project, fashion collection, or photo-shoot is disrespectful and unhelpful, especially when we look at the bigger picture."*

The bigger picture was her grand perception of white people oppressing others, as it always is, citing Julia writing at the website *à l'allure garçonnière*. Bastow also complained about white people using Navajo Indian styles.

Fashion house Victoria's Secret embraced Asia with its Go East collection in 2012. A floral and mesh camisole was meant to be "Eastern inspired," offering "your ticket to an exotic adventure."

"It's a troubling attempt to sidestep authentic representation and humanization of a culture and opt instead for racialized fetishizing against Asian women," complained website *Racialicious*. It accused Victoria's Secret of trying to express an essence of Asian identity, as if that were wrong. *"There's a long-standing trend to represent Asian women as hypersexualized objects of fantasy, so it's telling that none of the models wearing the Go East collection appear to be Asian."* Asian women should model our impressions of Asia, for us to know what's acceptable.

"Considering the complicated history of geishas," agreed website *Frisky*, for which I thought Japanese were more responsible than we were, *"repurposing the 'look' for a major corporation to sell as role-playing lingerie seems a bit tasteless."*

In 2014, allegations of racism led Sydney University to cancel the Mexican theme of its Christmas party. "I am Hispanic and I have some traditions from Mexican culture, and the vice chancellor's invite said 'bring your own sombreros and ponchos,' which reduces Mexican culture to just a costume," complained Eden Caceda, an office bearer with the university's Autonomous Collective Against Racism. "My family has a poncho and it is really important to us, and these people are treating it like a costume."

We can only tap into other people's cultures with their co-operation. Romance Was Born designers Anna Plunkett and Luke Sales collaborated with Bidjigal artist Esme Timbery for their 2009 and '10 range. In the 1980s, Linda Jackson worked with several Central Australian Aboriginal communities to create her textiles. *"See,"* wrote Clem Bastow, *"that's the great thing about fashion: those of us who love it know it doesn't have to be shallow, culturally insensitive or offensive. Involve yourself in cultural appropriation for the sake of being on-trend and you make yourself all of those things."*

It all seemed reasonable, except that we can't imagine owning our cultures. Cultural appropriation is another ideological wrong only white people commit.

Few images of old Australia were more iconic than the tuckerbags in which swagmen kept their food, few expressions more obviously Australian than "tucker," although multiculturalism meant my children had never before heard of tuckerbags or tucker until I mentioned them. They'd never heard the song of the dog on the tuckerbox, five miles from Gundagai.

Bakeries sell bread. All passers-by saw of the Tuckerbag Bakery in Marrickville, Sydney, was a name on a sign exuding Australia unchanged, but the company operating it was Project Paragon, headed by James Kwan. I read about it because a magistrate in 2009 said it showed "a reprehensible attitude to public health." Rat faeces invisible to customers were visible in the kitchens, with the unmistakable smell of rat urine.

Instead of emulating other races' ownership of their cultures, we throw ours open for everyone. We don't accuse other races of appropriating our cultures.

American architect Howard Garns invented the Number Place game in 1979, involving a partially completed nine-by-nine square grid that a player filled so that each column, row, and three-by-three box contained each of the nine numerical digits. After the game became popular in Japan in 1986, the publisher Nikoli renamed the game Sudoku. It became Japanese.

The culture we haven't abandoned, we've given away. From the awful Great War trenches, British soldier Hugh Lofting created the character Doctor Dolittle for his letters home to his children so they wouldn't be traumatised by war. When fighting finished, Lofting wrote a series of books and stories about the colourful Englishman who learned to talk to animals.

Dolittle was still English when Englishman Rex Harrison portrayed him in the 1967 film *Doctor Dolittle*. Thirty-one years later, long after Lofting had died, Eddie Murphy played the good doctor in another film of that name. The reviews I read of the film never mentioned it, but the doctor so clever he could converse with animals had become black.

Soon after the Second World War, Ian Fleming began writing novels about a fictional spy, James Bond, bravely fighting for Britain. By the 2008 film *Quantum of Solace*, Bond was no longer quintessentially British but indistinguishable from American Matt

Bourne or any other Western world-citizen spy. Aside from his accent, he could have been anyone. Little wonder then that, in 2013, Pierce Brosnan, who'd previously played Bond, endorsed Colin Salmon playing Bond. Salmon was black.

The secretary to Bond's boss M, Miss Eve Moneypenny, had already become black. Naomie Harris played her in the 2012 Bond film *Skyfall*.

We're not looking for heroes among our own, as other races like them among theirs. Richard Matheson's 1954 novel *I am Legend* appeared in several film forms with a white hero. In 2007, the hope of our world was black American Will Smith.

Exacting justice on the streets of New York, retired spy Robert McCall was white in the 1980s television series *The Equaliser*. In the 2014 film version, he was black.

The 2012 American television series *Elementary* was our postmodern impression of the great Sherlock Holmes. His friend and biographer Doctor Watson had become not just a woman. She was Chinese.

The West's loss of our cultural identities was never more obvious than in the 2011 film *Thor*, which I saw with my two youngest sons on Anzac Day that year. (Something seemed apt about seeing *Thor* on Anzac Day.) Derived from Marvel comics and inspired by Norse mythology, the Asgard world of great Viking Gods had become multiracial. The races far removed from a Scandinavian heritage weren't simply fellow Europeans, nor were they mere players in the crowd. Hogan, a charter member of the Warriors Three, had become Japanese, played by Tadanobu Asano.

The Norse God Heimdall inspired the comic book character of that name, the guardian of Asgard. Much like Malmö by 2011, Heimdall in the film was black, played by Idris Elba.

Kenneth Branagh also directed the 2015 American film *Cinderella*, inspired by an Italian folktale and recorded by Frenchman Charles Perrault in 1697. Not only did Branagh make medieval Europe comfortably multiracial, but the brave captain of the guards who overruled the wicked stepmother thereby allowing Cinderella and Prince Charming to reunite was black.

Other races don't just own their cultures and characters. They own what appear to be their cultures and characters.

Jake Gyllenhaal played the title character in the 2010 film *The Prince of Persia: The Sands of Time*. Twenty-two years old and calling herself an Iranian and Australian, writer Sara Haghdoosti accused Gyllenhaal of stealing her identity. Her identity was Persian. Anybody could play Doctor Dolittle or a Scandinavian warrior but only Persians could play Persians. The film wasn't based on Persian texts, but on a series of video games created by American Jewish designer Jordan Mechner.

With other races owning their cultures, can't white people own ours? Cultural ownership is natural, sensible even. Nobody need get uppity about races enjoying them, even incorporating them into their own. It's a compliment.

American Harold Gray's 1924 comic character Little Orphan Annie, who appeared in comics until 2010, was white with curly red hair. She remained so when Jewish lyricist Martin Charnin and composer Charles Strouse adapted the character for their 1977 musical *Annie* and in the 1982 film of that name. Becoming black in the 2014 film wasn't particularly interesting, until L'Sean Rinique Shelton raised seven thousand signatures to a petition complaining that the Target department store portrayed Annie as white in its December advertisements for a line of clothes the character inspired. Eighty-six years of being white in comics, a musical, and a film weren't enough to resist becoming black in the new film.

Target's defence wasn't that Annie was white, but that its advertisements included Annies of many races. Only white Annie upset Shelton.

In 2011, Marvel Comics responded to America's changing racial reality by announcing the killing of white, intellectual Peter Parker as Spider-Man. In his place came our new concept of hero: a half-black, half-Latino, new Spider-Man, Miles Morales. As if that weren't enough to demonstrate our inclusiveness, rumour was that Morales would be homosexual.

Not to be outdone, the following year DC Comics introduced superhero Simon Baz, a Muslim Lebanese from Detroit. No defender of the American way, DC Comic's chief creative officer Geoff Johns, from the Detroit area, was keen to show the impact of the September 2001 terrorist attacks on America. He wanted to describe the grief and prejudice suffered not by Americans, but by Arabs.

In 2013, Marvel Comics announced superheroine Ms Marvel was returning as sixteen-year-old Kamala Khan, the daughter of Pakistani immigrants living in Jersey City. Editor Sana Amanat called the character's stories dealing with superpowers, family expectations, religion, and adolescence a "desire to explore the Muslim American diaspora from an authentic perspective." Jake Gyllenhaal better not play her in a film.

12. WHO WE ARE

At our best, we've become trivial Europe, consumed by a sense of equality. So certain are we that all races are equal, it follows we've all achieved equally.

For a time through the late twentieth century, American educators tried to weigh equally the achievements of all races. That might seem nigh on impossible, but we strove in pursuit of the end. A mere drawing of a bird in a cave became evidence that primitive American Indians (as I recall) understood aerodynamics before Europeans did. We equated a returning boomerang with European aircraft to say the same of Aborigines. The more we valued other cultures for being better than ours, the less we needed such contrivances.

Without faith in our peoples, we cast our adoration elsewhere. After a year at Dongseo University, a blue-eyed, blond Brazilian named Max was so taken with Korea, he underwent more than ten surgical operations to appear Asian, dyed his hair black, wore dark contact lenses, and changed his name to Xiahn. He told readers of his Facebook computer page in 2014, *"you have to be who you wan to be."* It mattered more than being who he was.

Other white people aren't so extreme. My childhood neighbour Ryan at university studied economics and arts including, for the first time in his life, Asian studies. What excited him most was China. He abandoned studying economics (probably a sensible thing for anyone to do) to study all things Chinese: languages, history, art, and culture. He lived for a while in Hong Kong and Taiwan. At least he married a Canadian.

Greg, with whom I worked at Cement Australia, seems to have discovered Japan the same way. The boy from Wyong studied the Japanese language at university and set off to Japan. He went so far as to marry a woman from the land of his dreams, bringing her back to Australia.

All the glory of a race unacceptable if we felt it for our own becomes acceptable, even admirable, when we latch onto others;

our meekness turns back to pride. China is an obvious choice, with so numerous a people who've retained their self-confidence. For my eldest son's friend Michael, it was Japan.

East Asian countries are by no means the only options. Identifying with their chosen race, they're no longer post-racial white people. They're racial somebody else.

The most obvious differences between Greg and the Japanese were genes. The second was Japanese mistrust of China. Greg revered China too.

I doubt there are anywhere near so many Sinophiles among Japanese and Koreans, Japanophiles among Chinese and Koreans, or Koreaphiles among Japanese and Chinese as there are of each in the West. There might not be any. When my father and the elder of my two sisters visited China in 1985, a Chinese man explained to them the origin of the Japanese people. He said the Japanese were descended from a Chinese princess, who was raped by a monkey.

We don't value culture we know to be ours, because it's ours. Culture we like, we don't consider ours, but we could own our cultures, much as other races own theirs. A replica Pict pendant isn't mine just because I bought it in Inverness. It's mine whoever possesses each representation, because my ancient forebears were Picts.

In 1999, around the time we ceased being colleagues, I was in my friend Peter P's home (near the home in which I grew up). For the first time, I saw hanging the artwork he'd painted not for money, but because he wanted to paint. Downstairs was an easel on which his next work stood in progress. The strokes and imagery were uncommonly patient, thoughtful, and deep. Stepping from commerce to culture exuded more of him than anything he said or did at the office.

Peter's parents were Latvian. Thus Peter was Latvian (at least to our Jewish friend Ian Biner).

Never had I been colder than crossing a bridge over the frozen Daugava River, through the weekend I visited Riga between weeks working in Helsinki early in 1997. Most paintings offered for sale from painters and other hawkers in Europe were bland reproductions of local landmarks without people, but not one particular painting in Riga. Below the strong stone cathedral were images of people walking through the old part of town, dressed warmly from the cruel winter cold.

Latvians had treasured their nationhood when they broke away from the Soviet Union in 1991, reclaiming their independence. Sometime later they treasured their nationhood less. Their population fell steadily, and the people who'd fought to escape the crumbling Soviet Union freely joined the rich European Union in 2004. Her new economy collapsed late in the decade, as such economies were collapsing throughout much of the West. All the while, that painting from Riga hung from a wall in my home.

Cultures reveal us. Commerce and ideologies conceal us.

The Austrian city of Graz was proud of her emigrant son Arnold Schwarzenegger for being a famous bodybuilder, actor, and then governor of California, but by 2005 Graz was the first "city of human rights," determined to advocate the city council's vision of a global good at the expense of kinship. Late at night, it removed Schwarzenegger's name from the local sports stadium because, as California governor, he'd refused to spare from lawful execution black American Stanley Tookie Williams, who'd murdered four people. Graz City Council opposed the death penalty not just in Graz, Austria, and Europe but everywhere. Europeans trusted Williams to have rehabilitated himself, as we trust other races to do.

Graz City Council's vision wasn't post-racial but racial, for any race but its own. Council considered renaming the stadium after the Crips, the criminal gang Williams founded, or Hakoah, a Jewish sports club banned after Nazi German dictator Adolf Hitler annexed Austria in 1938. It didn't think of naming the stadium for Austrians associated with Graz, such as astronomer Johannes Kepler, physicist Erwin Schrödinger, or conductor Karl Böhm.

It became boring U.P.C. – Arena, although a newspaper poll found seventy percent of Graz's townspeople wanted Schwarzenegger's name on the stadium. "One stands by a friend and a great citizen of our city," protested mayor Siegfried Nagl, "and does not drag his name through the mud even when there is a difference of opinion."

Schwarzenegger played Douglas Quaid in the 1990 American film *Total Recall*. "You are what you do," the mutant Kuato told him in the movie. "A man is defined by his actions, not his memory." Stripped of all recollection, Quaid never learnt whether his life was a dream or real.

We trust cinema screens. Few characters fill our screens more than comic book heroes.

Bruce Wayne was young, white, and rich, but also alone, secretly doing good deeds people didn't appreciate, and sorely troubled by the deaths of his parents. "Bruce," Rachel Dawes told him in the 2005 film *Batman Begins*, "deep down you may still be that great kid you used to be, but it's not who you are underneath, it's what you do that defines you." By the end of the film, he agreed.

Wayne's identity was Batman. It was a mask.

Kuato was wrong. Dawes was wrong.

Through the year of my thirtieth birthday, 1992, I attended two seminars in an industrial estate at St Leonards. They were tax-deductible.

For some participants, they were work-related education. The Westpac trading bank and other companies referred employees there, although not the company at which I worked at the time.

The second seminar filled five days. The seminar leaders insisted we undertake not to drink alcohol (or have any sexual experiences) through those days to keep our minds clear, even when we adjourned for dinner among the nearby restaurants each evening. When a restaurant hand told a small group of us at the door there was no room to seat us, a woman among us was appalled. "I'd never let a customer get away like that," she told us, we men and women convulsed with commerce and our careers. Every customer was profit. Her thoughts of business never wavered.

Conducting my long seminar sessions was a fair-haired American, Cynthia. All but one of the seminar leaders were American, as I imagine were almost all the leaders at the plethora of such seminars popular at the time. Americans were the missionaries for individualism.

Cynthia's self-confidence and purpose-laden suit and skirt made her seem taller than she really was. "What you think of me is none of my business," was her expression for the idea we individuals needn't care what other individuals thought of us. ("Sticks and stones may break my bones, but names will never hurt me," expressed a little something of the same idea: another adage from the past we no longer uttered.) At a time people were increasingly becoming quick to feel offence, her words were rather refreshing. They were also a rejection of social mores, an assertion of our individualism.

Most memorable were Cynthia's words during an exchange between her and Stacey. Perhaps becoming tired, Cynthia said to Stacey: "Who you are is more important than anything you'll ever do."

They were remarkably profound words, particularly coming from an American. Implicitly acknowledging how much the seminars were carefully prepared, Cynthia said later those words "just came to" her. Surprised to have said them, she must have recognised how profound they were. Through subsequent seminar sessions, Cynthia repeated them several times over, as Americans do.

The most obvious things we ever did were the careers that seemed to have brought many of the participants before her, but Cynthia could have said the same of anything we would ever own or believe. We think so much of our careers and causes, glibly presuming to know who we happen to be. More important than the work that we do, wealth that we have, or beliefs that we hold, are the people we are.

Through my first seminar, I had become friends with an accountant Christine Fraser. Christine talked outside the seminars of finding the pixie within her.

Fifteen years after I last saw Christine, I recalled my time with her. She came to mind because of a pretty woman forty-one years old I never met, and of whom I had never heard until I saw a newspaper photograph and caption speaking of fairies. The more I read the more I wanted to learn about Milli O'Nair.

Milli O'Nair had done many things unimaginable for me, including laughter yoga and Buddhism. She had lived in a residential community dedicated to meditation and sustainable development. She painted children's faces, tended to a fairy stall at local markets, and dressed as a fairy for children's birthday parties. Becoming a non-violent communication coach and teacher, she had travelled around eastern Australia, planning to change the world.

Had Milli O'Nair been the name to which she was born, I could have imagined her fair-complexioned forebears with mine on that distant Emerald Isle, Ireland. Instead, she had been Milarepa Hooper: Milarepa the name of a Tibetan yogi and poet a thousand years earlier, which said as much as anything about how estranged her parents were from their English origins. With identity so fickle and money so enticing, she chose the name Milli O'Nair to express what she aspired to be: a millionaire. A million dollars seemed a strange thing for a fairy to want.

Two days before that newspaper photograph and caption, on the morning of Mother's Day 2009, she had been riding her bicycle along a narrow bridge on the Pacific Highway a little north of Byron Bay, headed to her mother's home. Mina Nashed was driving a truck, but said later he nodded briefly to sleep. His truck struck her bicycle, killing her instantly and hurtling her fairy body from the bridge onto heavy scrub and railway tracks.

Milli O'Nair's life had been estranged from mine, and yet I felt sadder than I felt about other strangers dying. I assumed she had no children to be travelling alone to her mother on Mother's Day, although she was engaged to be married.

Who we are does not mean being only an individual. It means being part of a family, clan, ethnicity, and race.

Only we, whose ancestors came from Europe from where fairy tales also came, produce people like Milli O'Nair and Christine Fraser. Other races have their tales, while we produced fairies. We could seem so playful and whimsical, but by the end of the twentieth century, seemed lost, wanting to hide.

13. ART

Unable to appropriate other people's cultures should mean we express ourselves with our cultures, but asserting our cultures we consider culturally insensitive to others. What remains for us is our cultureless, ideological postmodernism, along with shopping and work.

At the time of the float of Holyman Limited in 1994, employees could charge taxi fares to their employer by completing and signing small paper dockets that we left with the driver. The dockets included space for the employee to describe the purpose of the trip, ensuring it related to work. Reuben described the purpose of one trip between Redfern and Sydney for which he and I were both passengers as being "*another boring meeting.*"

Some years earlier, Reuben and I shared a business trip to Melbourne. Before flying back to Sydney, he led us into a brief visit to the National Gallery of Victoria.

Through the decade we worked together, Reuben's passion for painting and drawing grew. Feeling free at Holyman, he stood his sketches and watercolours on the floor against the walls around his office.

Reuben's weekly art classes involved models posing naked or, when one model failed to arrive, a fellow student whipping off her clothes. Our multilingual secretary Liz (university qualified, with an arts degree) was somewhat taken aback when Reuben contemplated her posing for his class. She let the idea lapse. Amidst long negotiations for the acquisition of Union Shipping costing more than a hundred million dollars, Reuben told a senior male executive of another multinational company he needed to leave early for his art class that evening, unless the executive was willing to take off his clothes.

What once surprised or annoyed me came to inspire me, without suggesting anyone undress. It's a rare man who'll reduce his income and workload to spend a day each week painting, as did one law firm partner (said my friend Rehana in 2001).

I can't paint, but I can admire: fine craftwork by people I don't know. I pause before paintings by artists who've died.

Losing sight of our forebears, we've lost sight of our artists and thus of our art. "The aim of art is to represent not the outward appearance of things," said Greek philosopher Aristotle in the third century Before Christ, "but their inward significance." The State Library of Victoria felt his words still pertained when it displayed them in 2011.

Representing inward significance wasn't at the expense of outward appearance, not in classical Europe. Hanging from our dining room wall is a colourful image of a Victorian-age woman, tending to a patterned porcelain cup of tea atop a similar saucer. She's adorned with frills of white and blue, with a white scarf around her fair hair and skin very white.

She's pretty because she was pretty in 1855 and because Alfred Ernest Owen bought a wealth of pristine lithographs and stored them inside a vault in his moated mansion at New Hall, before dying in 1929 or thereabouts. The lithographs remained undiscovered until 1982. If the person finding them hadn't cared about art, or known of people caring enough to buy them, they would've been discarded.

I bought my lithograph from a gallery in Plymouth in 1993. I hope my children treasure the art around our home after my wife and I die.

At our heart was Christian tradition. The richest and most meaningful art I can see every week of my life are the paintings shining through our parish Anglican and family Uniting church windows. Standing in muted light, gazing through stained glass at Christ with His Disciples, I am in Christendom.

Our arts venerated people and God, but near the rear of our parish Anglican church is a pair of postmodern windows, where the colours are jagged and imagery unclear. The artist was lazy, the work in a rush. If Christ is there, He hides in the shapes. If they weren't in a church, I wouldn't imagine them being Christian. I'm not sure they are, devoid of human image. Artistic relativism refuses to assert God any more than anything else previously part of our culture. Unrecognisable stained glass glorifies nothing at all.

If not to God, we in our great periods at least reached above ourselves, drawing from strengths we sensed within us or to which we aspired. Our oil paintings were of beautiful, proud people in pretty, old places. From the turn of the nineteenth century, the statues of handsome heroes and heroines in Kings Park, Perth, acclaimed individuals and thus all of us: our people and thus people.

A hundred years later, our artistry lacks optimism, our art no longer glorious. Around Western cities are occasional figures of men and women leaning against walls, sitting on benches, and standing at bus stops. A figure on the Perth business district footpaths of 2010 stood on his hands. Modern man in statuette is the commonplace in cast bronze: a rudimentary realism, so crude as to be lifelike. Their ordinariness intends merely to amuse and distract people noticing them: equality rather than exaltation. Purportedly representing every man or woman, they represent none.

Even the sculpture of Septimus Roe, who died in 1878, seemed strangely nondescript in the streets of postmodern Perth: a little smaller than ordinary. Heroes and heroines have become rare in our art, because they've become rare in our culture.

Conveying no sense of people or God, our art doesn't glorify either. Perhaps the artist feels glorified.

Few passers-by pause to study shapes of rocks, bronze, and steel our artists title man, woman, or whatever, with prefixes or other descriptions to explain what the sculptors say they represent. Without titles and captions, we wouldn't know. The figures are forms we call people, without eyes, noses, and mouths in faces once real. What remains are whatever impression each person imagines.

It's abstract. Joseph Mallord William Turner and William Turner of Oxford didn't need titles to tell audiences they were looking at scenery.

For all the wealth of stone streets and grand piazzas I've seen in Italy, I've never seen Florence. Inspired by Christianity, the maestro Michelangelo carved his masterpiece *David* from marble other artisans considered useless. He didn't need a caption.

Our artists began turning away from traditional styles before the Great War. Those who couldn't find comfort in classical art after the war embraced ever more modernist abstractions.

Hanging from our lounge room wall is a printed reproduction of a painting that hangs in the Australian War Memorial, Canberra, which Will Longstaff painted in 1927 after attending the dedication of the Menin Gate memorial arch at Ypres in Belgium. Half a million men died there through four years of fighting, almost ninety thousand bodies disintegrated in mud, in an area of just twenty-five square kilometres. Walking uneasily, not really marching, past the gate lit up at night are half a million ghostly skeletons not laid to rest.

We called it modernism when we pushed aside our European heritage. We called it postmodernism when we pushed aside everything.

Art has become no less political than anything else. Our friend Peta's daughter Elisa painted three portraits demonstrating different attitudes to school for her Higher School Certificate at Riverside Girls High School in 2014, but her instructor advised her that examiners liked multicultural themes. She thus doctored the portrait of one student to appear Asian. She doctored another, the dedicated student, to appear Aboriginal.

For her major work, my middle-born daughter painted something beautiful in watercolour. Her teacher awarded her forty out of fifty marks, but told my daughter she would have awarded more had the painting a concept.

"The *Mona Lisa* didn't have a concept," I scoffed, when my daughter mentioned it to me. "*Whistler's Mother* didn't have a concept."

By concept, an ideology of inclusion would do. My daughter said later she'd have fared better had her pictures promoted multiculturalism. Had Leonardo da Vinci painted the *Mona Lisa* in 2016, he'd have needed to make her an immigrant.

Our arts no longer exalt us. They exalt everyone else.

The New South Wales Department of Education and Training annual calendars aren't concerned with cultural excellence but diversity. The 2009 calendar included my eldest daughter's painting of the sun. "*My work is inspired by the importance of the sun in Aboriginal culture*," she wrote, having been taught more about Aboriginal than European art. "*Blending pinks and blues with the earth colours of traditional Aboriginal art symbolises the different cultures of our society.*"

The last local cultures in Europe's former colonies are indigenous. Without obvious sense of the irony, the foyer of Sydney law firm Gilbert & Tobin's offices displayed Aboriginal funeral art.

We're less interested in Europe's indigenous cultures. It's hard to imagine fifteenth-century Italian painter Sandro Botticelli blowing paints around the outlines of his hands, pressed against rock walls and tree trunks.

No longer is there the adage, "I don't know much about art, but I know what I like." Instead is the adage, "I don't know much about art, but I know what I paid."

Wayne, a human resources general manager with whom I worked, bought huge paintings overseas costing more than most cars, packed into crates for delivery to his office. Paying money to art dealers is a pleasure, while evading tax paid to governments is a game. He told me the crates were labelled with falsely low values for the art (reducing the import duties he paid), although he might have just wanted me to think the paintings cost more than they did. Who could tell?

Art is a wonderful way for anyone with too much money to spend vast amounts of it; the most we appreciate of our art is being rich enough to buy it. We need only to check the price tag to know whether it's quality or not. The more expensive art is, the better artistically it must be.

In 2013, hanging from the walls of the K&L Gates public seminar room were paintings representing huge melted paddle pop ice creams. At least I could see what they were.

We like art more than artists, but ours is the art that monetary artists working efficiently make: maximum output for minimal cost. Trying to earn income from art and as much as they can, they use lines of rapid factory production. Traditional art's intricacies too often left artists dying poor, before their paintings became rich.

Culture embraces creativity, but ours is commercial creativity. Western culture is a commercial culture.

With dedicated roles and specialisation, creativity and imagination serve commercial objectives. They're something for films, psychology for selling, and innovation for new product lines: the province of marketers and advertisers in realms of deep people teams. They're something to buy in a gift for someone who'd not imagined such a gift. They're artists' works exhibited on public gallery walls, making money from their profession saying they never would. Few of us pay much attention.

Classical art focused upon the subject and viewer. Modern art cares only about the artist, be it a job for income or ideologically explicit.

Art is a business much like any other, with consumers even less exacting about quality than we are with other consumption. Busy people want decorations for their offices and homes they needn't waste time to study.

For people not just walking past, art is contemplative. Self-indulgent spectators with time to contemplate ponder themselves.

Mellow lines of abstract with strange, coloured shapes don't need to mean anything. Rarely does our art portray people, at least people identifiable as people (unless the consumer commissions a portrait of himself), when we're trying to appeal to the world. Geometry overwhelms humanity.

Even our portraiture can be without people. Tim Storrier won the 2012 Archibald Prize for his self-portrait: a figure with spectacles, but no face. The artist's face was on a small piece of paper hovering in the air, at which his dog stared.

Prizes are money for art that's too hard to sell (although nothing inflates the price of art more than experts conferring a prize on the artist). The Turner Prize, presented by the Tate Gallery and first awarded in 1984, is Great Britain's leading prize for contemporary art. The 2001 prize was awarded to a pair of flashing lights in an empty room. Abstract nothingness prevailed over an array of disparate objects filling a dusty storeroom.

Our rooms are empty. Our people have gone.

From cultural nihilism came human nihilism. Men and women vanish from our consciousness, in spite of the consumers around.

In presenting the 2001 Turner Prize, the singer Madonna called everyone a winner, rejected the idea there is a best of anything, and reduced every award to a matter of opinion: cultural relativism. What matters in our individualist West is our individual response, which is more emotional than intellectual, as indeed we are. The expletive deleted from press reports of her speech suggested she lauded political correctness over honesty, as we do.

Our postmodern arts are the arts of equality. No one feels hurt, but when everyone wins, nobody wins. We don't even try. Our forebears knew ours to be the finest arts on earth, but they'd gone to war. Our rejection of our cultural heritage is our rejection of excellence.

Not everyone's a winner, not all the time, in our rejection of our cultural heritage. In spite of her stage name, Madonna sang 'Live to Tell' on a crucifix while wearing a crown of thorns, during a visit to

Moscow in 2006.

Finding new ways to represent nothingness became difficult. The 2008 Sydney Biennale included an old film of chickens being decapitated, because a modern recording might distress visitors. It also included a dead horse hanging from the ceiling, although organisers assured people that the horse died of natural causes.

Unlike other vocations, artists in our postmodern West don't need to achieve a threshold of quality. They need only call themselves artists.

In May 2012, artist Amelia Hitchcock dragged a block of ice dyed pink and weighing twenty-five kilograms from Massey University to the Square in Palmerston North, New Zealand. "This ice block is a statement about temporal relationships," she explained, "…how things change over time." Each kilogram represented a year of her life. (It must have been a fulsome life.)

At least Hitchcock stayed awake. In March 2013, Scottish actress Tilda Swinton spent six hours apparently sleeping in a glass box in the Museum of Modern Art, New York. She'd previously performed her living art at the Serpentine Gallery in Hyde Park, London in 1995 and the Museo Barracco in Rome in 1996. Swinton and her collaborator Cornelia Parker called her performance: 'The Maybe.'

More than simply self-indulgent, it was all so transitory. We feel for a moment, leaving nothing behind.

Biblical stories and Christian tradition inspired much of our greatest art, while I can't imagine Leonardo da Vinci dragging a block of ice through Milan. He didn't need to name a good day's sleep, 'maybe.' We can still stand in awe before his *Last Supper* fresco and *Mona Lisa* paintwork.

Whatever critics and audiences thought of Sala Murat's artwork, valued at ten thousand euros, in his exhibition in the province of Bari, Italy opening in February 2014, a cleaner thought the newspaper and cardboard with biscuit pieces scattered across the floor were rubbish. She threw them out. Lorenzo Roca, from cleaning firm Chiarissima, said she was "just doing her job."

City marketing commissioner Antonio Maria Vasile wasn't fazed. He said "this is all about the artists who have been able to better interpret the meaning of contemporary art, which is to interact with the environment."

We call our contemporary art modern as if other art wasn't and postmodern as if anything could be, but it's easy to see the loss of ourselves in the emptiness of our art. When we were European, we had art. At best, ours is now art without beauty: respite from the world. At worst, it's art without people: all that remains after the ghosts of Menin Gate pass.

14. ARCHITECTURE AND DESIGN

Perhaps once in my decade working in North Sydney, did I pause on the Miller Street footpath just before midday to look up at the clock tower of the Tower Square arcade. A short procession of mechanical figures, including a cow and medieval people, twirled around slowly with music, much like the figures I often admired among the elegance of old Europe in 1986. I know of nothing else like it in Australia.

Many of my colleagues with whom I worked simply worked and dined when they travelled on company business, seeing nothing worthwhile. Some of us did more. In places I visited, I inspected artistic, architectural, religious, literary, and historical attractions. I led my accountant friend Peter to historical sites in Lisbon such as the Belem Tower and Jerónimos Monastery in December 1997, while ensuring the eating and drinking he wanted were in venues from which I could admire the view, such as the café atop the Santa Justa lift finished in 1902.

"Tonight we live and eat Portugal," I told the waiter or waitress at the Timpanas restaurant that Saturday night, in my determination to experience Portuguese culture. Peter imagined the staff then offloading any old rubbish onto me, trusting them it was Portuguese. I hope he was wrong.

When our people mattered so much, so did the buildings we made. We now think less about castles, than we think about gift shops.

John Bradfield, who oversaw the construction of the Sydney Harbour Bridge, remarked that history judged civilisations by the works they left behind (according to the Pymble Players recital in our parish Anglican church cemetery during the 2013 fête). Only European peoples could've built such a bridge in 1932, or even now, spanning a great harbour from each side and meeting perfectly in the centre. Bradfield chose granite for the pylons, so they would stand forever.

We produced, seeing as much beauty in what we created as in

what we did not. Styles evolved, while being European.

There was a time our buildings reached not just for the sky, but for the soul. Tall towers could be grand, as is the Empire State Building, New York, opened in 1931. Our cities were fine places to live.

The du Pont Hotel opened in Wilmington before the Great War. Its restaurant and bars' rich shining stone columns was commercial imperialism to be sure, exuding confidence, grandeur, and fun.

The worst thing about the Perth Council House in 2010 wasn't its ugliness, especially compared with the lovely old Town Hall. It was the realisation that more recent buildings were worse. Our refusal to assert our cultures means our buildings become cultureless.

An article in the *New South Wales Law Society Journal*, in the first decade of the twenty-first century, calmly explained that our courts and other public buildings need to ensure no culture prevails over another. (Multiculturalism is predicated upon it.) The rest of our buildings share the same presumption. Our countries formerly teeming with culture become bland.

I never understood university students describing the bleak, brown concrete block of the New South Wales Institute of Technology building in Sydney as fascist, until I worked in a commonplace city office. (Those students presumed only fascists were totalitarian. If the building were communist, it would have been blander still and probably collapsing.) Our buildings replaced confidence with arrogance, grandeur with ego, fun with power. Rarely is money wasted on motifs, colonnades, or sentiment, each of which exudes something of culture. What remains is architecture without elegance.

We're consumed by creating the tallest, but not the most beautiful, buildings. Unwilling to express beauty because beauty is culturally sensitive, stark and fierce are fine.

We're never more masculine than in the tall buildings in which we increasingly live and work, above crowded shopping arcades and fitted gymnasiums. People we don't know come to clean, watering our flower-box plants so we don't risk dirtying our factory-office fingers.

Our masculinity satisfied, the accountants in urban design pursue function. No longer offering ornamental columns and arches, our commercial buildings are venues for purpose. In hot climes, buildings have excess glass to reflect away sunlight, minimising air-conditioning costs. Being self-interested individuals, the neighbours don't matter. Reflected sunlight heats the surrounding buildings, increasing their air-conditioning costs. Being equally self-interested, the surrounding glass buildings shine the heat back.

Corporations are no places for dreamers, unless the company business is selling those dreams. Consumers buy the dreams that we want.

Beauty is a cost we forgo. Away from local council concerns in the fields of south Queensland, the Millmerran Power Station saved itself the expense of installing cladding and walls. Exposed for the cows and farmers to see was an engineer's delight of dark pipes and furnaces.

Much of our history has gone. Opened in 1975, Old Sydney Town recreated our First Settlement a little north of Sydney. It closed in 2003. Opened in 1869, the Zig Zag Railway was an extraordinary achievement traversing the Blue Mountains until superseded in 1910. Restored in 1967, it closed in 2012.

Our forebears couldn't imagine us neglecting our architectural heritage, let alone destroying it. At night, vandals break through wire fences sealing old buildings, spraying them with scrawls only they understand. We have no sense of being a people owning a heritage or of the beauty they're wrecking. The *North Shore Times* newspaper merrily reported local parliamentarian Jonathan O'Dea organising a group of residents to clean the old Killara post office after Ku-ring-gai Council and the building owner refused to remove the graffiti. The graffiti soon returned.

Graffiti was initially confined to public and commercial buildings. By 2013, it soiled house walls and signs in the suburb in which I live. Without culture, our streets are just traffic signs, advertisements, and graffiti. If Western multicultural individualism has a moniker, then it's graffiti.

If we want land, we'll demolish our heritage before we restore it, whenever we can. The few people outside Eastern Europe who noticed were horrified when Romanian communist dictator Nicolae Ceaușescu ordered the demolition of more than a fifth of Bucharest to build his Paris of the East. Yet we allow developers to demolish huge numbers of old homes in our cities for the money they make building bland blocks of apartments. At least Ceaușescu pursued some vision of beauty.

My wife believed the prestigious private girls' school at which she'd taught was demolishing its beautiful old boarding house in 2013, because boarders coming from Asia wouldn't like it. We eradicate our heritage to accommodate others. We do so for money. In its place would come a postmodern monstrosity, like the adjacent senior school studies centre. If Asian students can't study among their cultures, they study among none.

Other races aren't so reticent about expressing their cultures as we are about expressing ours, even in what were our countries. If they're not merrily building new temples and everything else in their architectural styles, they're superseding ours.

The structure housing the Taoist deity of Wong Tai Sin downstairs and Buddhist temple of Kwan Yin upstairs had all the style I'd expect East Asian temples to have, but this was in Summer Hill, Sydney. Nothing in the photograph I saw revealed its history but, back in the 1920s, presumably with European columns and an Australian European style, it was a Masonic temple.

Other races don't care about our architectural and engineering history. They care about theirs. So do we. In 2012, Wyong Shire Council excitedly announced the building of a new theme park near what had been Old Sydney Town, including a replica of gates to the Forbidden City in Beijing and a nine-storey Chinese temple.

God inspired some of the greatest art and architecture ever produced, forged in beauty and skill with majesty, wonder, and awe. Most churches in which I've spent time have steeples bringing heaven a little closer to earth. Coventry Cathedral was a major architectural and artistic achievement, before German aircraft bombed it almost to oblivion during World War II. A little shell remained, for my girlfriend and me to walk through one rainy day, 1986.

Beside that ruin, so painfully in place, was the uninspiring new Coventry Cathedral. Big wasn't beautiful, huge wasn't impressive. The new cathedral was design without décor, dedicated more to a fear of war than love for God or for peace. Visitors paid for everything, and almost everything was for sale. We don't want great architecture anymore, for fear we'll lose it again.

"It's not the building, it's the people," complained students when the University of New South Wales planned to erect several new steel and glass buildings a few years after I'd finished studying there. They wanted more money spent on them. Churches make the same excuses for building postmodern churches indistinguishable from houses, conference centres, and warehouses next door. The facilities around us are soulless. We're equally soulless.

We might study the architecture and artwork of old European cathedrals, paying admission prices to examine tombs and memorials and to explore naves and deep crypts without parallel elsewhere. Few of us treat them as ours. My girlfriend with whom I holidayed in Europe in 1986 and China in 1988 was Roman Catholic. "I can go into any Catholic church in the world," said her mother, "and feel at home."

I felt at home in the many churches we visited, even in Coventry, and not only those Roman Catholic. I wasn't at home visiting a synagogue in Prague. Seven years later, a cathedral that had become an Istanbul mosque was no longer our home. The mosques we visited when I took my father to Malaysia two years after that never had been our home. In a Kuala Lumpur church built during British rule, we were at home.

We're only at home where we feel it, and not always then. Too few of us feel it.

The first Sunday in November 2010, sitting in the upstairs tea room after the five thirty service at our parish Anglican church, Kat and I talked about travel to Europe. I mentioned the splendour of St Peter's Square in Rome, but Kat had no sense of the glory. She saw only the system of people paying indulgences from which the Roman Catholic Church earned income (funding the Renaissance, before Christian merchant benefactors took up the cause).

I suggested to Kat we shouldn't impose our thinking on people so long ago. Those indulgences were like fines: a sense of atonement or righting a wrong. We could look upon modern-day tithing or offertory the same way.

Kat was unmoved. She went onto complain about the church in which we sat inviting parishioners to donate money to restore our church organ. Were our churches any cultural heritage but ours, we'd rush to save them. They're not.

"In my observation," I told her, "money spent on church organ funds isn't money that would've otherwise gone to the poor, but would've been spent on washing machines and refrigerators."

Kat was, as always, unmoved. With us was Feng.

I think I mentioned the need for a church building, before Kat or Feng inquired, "Do we need a church building?"

"What are we going to do?" I asked. "Sit under a tree?"

Feng nodded thoughtfully. The church wasn't his heritage.

Kat's family had worshiped there for generations. Her grandfather still alive had been the rector for decades. A stained-glass window was dedicated in her grandmother's name. She nevertheless didn't recognise the church as her heritage. To my facetious inquiry whether we should dismantle it all and sit under a tree, she replied, "We could."

15. HOMES AND HOUSES

The strength of a nation is derived from the integrity of its homes, said Chinese philosopher Confucius more than two thousand years ago. When Europeans were empires, we built for empires. When we were nations, we built for eternity.

We long ago withdrew from most of the countries we colonised, leaving behind the structures of civilisation still used there: great public buildings, roads and railways, water systems and farming. In the Cameron Highlands near Kuala Lumpur, the loveliest hotels and restaurants in 1995 were relics of English Tudor style.

The most interesting hotel in Bangkok is the Oriental, where writers Somerset Maugham, Noel Coward, and James Michener stayed. In 2006, I only visited.

Away from the most devoted of government patronage or tourist incomes, other vestiges of empire greyed. The European quarters of Shanghai had dulled, when I saw them in 1988. The heritage isn't theirs to preserve.

Our homes and suburbs had strength with architectural style: palaces where we had space, terraced homes where we didn't. Built in 1908, Craig-y-Mor in Wolseley Road, Point Piper enjoyed high ceilings, bay windows, arches, and a central courtyard with colonnades, but a hundred years later wasn't officially listed as a heritage asset. Zeng Wei, known also as Arthur, and his wife Jiang Mei bought it in 2008 preparing to move with their two sons to Sydney. To build the house they wanted, they demolished Craig-y-Mor.

Our heritage isn't simply for sale. It's for demolition.

The fourth Friday of October 2009 at a dinner we both attended, Barry Taylor and I talked about the beautiful old homes being demolished to make way for concrete apartment blocks, although he didn't care. "It's not happening in my street," he explained. Even if it were happening in his street, he wouldn't have cared, provided his street was long enough so that he couldn't see the blocks from his home.

Our houses are more Western than we realise. In 2009, Aboriginal leader Rosalie Kunoth-Monks complained that building houses for indigenous Aborigines was our latest attempt to assimilate them into white society.

Big, wide Australasia and the Americas provided us space for comfortable homes on large parcels of land, quarter-acre blocks even, where we played outdoors with our neighbours. By 2011, Campement Urbain artist Sylvie Blocher complained that low-density sprawl was a problem for public transport. When listing the problems of Penrith, she also included monocultural spaces dead at night, seeing something wrong with Australians headed home earlier than Asians, Africans, and Islanders wandering the streets.

Most telling of all, she mentioned social dislocation. We've suffered such dislocation with multiculturalism, which no number of sushi bars overcome.

The places in which we live (like those in which we work and shop) are increasingly matters of economic efficiency, not human fulfilment. We're becoming urban beasts confined to concrete boxes high in the air, standing in city pillars among streets of more pillars: shoebox apartments for which workers and consumers pay too much money and from which we want to spend days and evenings away. They're projects for profit upon construction and sale. They're then commercial operations for lease and for living.

If it all sounds like Hong Kong then it should. While we refused to assert our cultures by 2014, property developers in Sydney were designing apartment buildings catering to Feng Shui and other Chinese tastes.

Trying to preserve the traditional homes of red bricks, slate roofs, and wide verandas among several suburbs surrounding ours are organisations with names usually beginning with claims to be Friends. We might not have friends, but suburbs and the municipal environment do.

The elegant old homes we are trying to preserve are not our own. They are our neighbours'. They are houses we see through our clean lounge room windows, short enough not to shade the sun from our gardens. They are houses we pass along our late afternoon strolls.

Residential neighbours have become like everyone else, passing through other people's lives. We no longer look over our fences to wish them good day, but to check they are not breaching by-laws. Given one neighbour my family and I suffered, we should have checked.

Commercially driven fashion decries accumulation as clutter. Spaciousness encourages more purchases. Something new is acquired. Something else is discarded. Homes become minimalist. Hoarding becomes mental illness.

Culture and taste have become like everything else: consumable, and buyable. When we without confidence in our culture want décor, we buy magazines or hire people to decorate. Décor is anything that isn't primarily functional. Fashion matters too much for us to trust our judgements; our tastes are those that experts tell us they are. We might be experts in our chosen vocation, but not in what combinations of colours, patterns, and materials are fashionable and what aren't.

There is a reason some styles are classic and timeless. They look nice. Beauty doesn't cease to be beauty with the passage of time, but fashions have little, if anything, to do with beauty.

Fashion demands change, again driving consumers to discard the old and purchase anew. We don't care if our clothes and everything else don't last long. We don't keep them long anyway.

Not to be fashionable would mean to be poor. We don't want to seem poor.

My sense of tastefully decorating our traditionally styled home was to tile only halfway up the cement-rendered brick bathroom walls. "No," snapped the Teranova Ceramics tile shop manager, an Italian, in Willoughby. "That looks like you ran out of money!"

The Turramurra Tilecraft shop franchisee, a German, assured me the coloured grout he was selling lasted forever. Later I learnt that it faded over time. "No," he insisted, shaking his head.

"I heard it fades over ten or fifteen years," I explained.

"Who knows where any of us are in fifteen years? We could all be dead!"

Forever in the West is just fifteen years. It can be much less. The Turramurra Tilecraft shop closed a year or so later.

Like all else in our short Western lives, we no longer build for eternity. We build for the moment.

We feel no sentiment for our homes, be they houses or countries. The homes we now build need only last the short time before we sell them and go. Without races and countries, we have nothing to endure. Our single-person homes are no less transient than our single-person lives: décor without durability.

With rapid construction, Toronto defines our dream of the future: a multiracial metropolis of poorly built apartments. In 2011, developer David House (that really was his name) of Earth Development called the glass-walled towers "throwaway buildings," because of the problems he forecast within fifteen years after construction.

16. MUSIC

"There'll always be an England," sung Vera Lynn through World War II, "and England shall be free." I'm not so sure about either, but she had a qualification. "If England means as much to you, as England means to me."

The boundaries of Europe and pan-Europe change. They no longer include Anatolia: what we now call Turkey. Turkey and Israel (a Jewish country among other Semitic countries) nominate performers for the annual Eurovision Song Contest but for that matter, so does Azerbaijan. In 2015, so did Australia. The West never sets our nets wider than when we're in the mood for music.

The Eurovision Song Contest isn't about music, anyway. It's about multiculturalism.

Asserting our cultures in our countries didn't used to be a problem, for us or for anyone else. While the Second World War raged in Europe, Jewish songwriter Irving Berlin composed 'White Christmas,' without explicit reference to God but still something Roman Catholic Bing Crosby could sing. The whiteness referred to snow.

"There are a lot of bad things about working here," muttered Peter, the Holyman Limited finance manager, the last Tuesday in May 1997, "but one good thing is you can do what you want."

Expressing that more profoundly than anyone else, without needing to realise it, was Reuben. The day after Peter made his remark, unaware that he had, Reuben invited us all to a concert at his Uniting church in Lane Cove that Saturday night. There, he would sing.

Reuben retired when dismissed from that company and moved to Kiama, with enough money to ski, walk through forests, paint, sing, and travel. No company at which I've worked since then has appointed someone with his character and breadth of interests so senior an executive. Those companies only dismissed them, but that's unnatural selection.

Rarely have I enjoyed an evening and been moved more than

the Saturday I spent with some of my children in near-darkness at our parish Anglican church. Not far from the old stone chapel, beneath the softly lit, stained-glass windows, the angelic church organist Jane plied her harp. Half a dozen or so child flautists and other musicians, most of them girls, stood before the stone altar, trying their best to play old Gaelic tunes. I don't think the tunes were Christian. They were more ancient than that.

Without much imagination, the setting could have been anytime through the past two thousand years. The supple light could've come from candles, casting flutters of shadows in the chipped away stones. It could've been Ireland, exuding eternity.

The music was more than just wistful. It was mine: my love among the shadows.

We can appreciate other people's music without thinking it's ours. As good as any I've heard has been Paul Simon's writing and Art Garfunkel's singing, but their Jewish music isn't mine. Had they never drawn upon English folk music, I might never have heard 'Scarborough Fair.' That music is mine. I'm forever grateful they performed it so well.

The best of our songs are poems with melody: poetry's chance to endure. The complimentary poster picturing the *Magical Mystery Tour* bus and a few sights from Beatles landmarks in Liverpool wasn't really worth framing to hang on a wall in our home, but it hangs there anyway.

I didn't learn of René Descartes from my philosophy lectures during my postgraduate university studies of business. I learnt of him through the British 'Philosopher's Drinking Song' of 1973.

Increasingly since the 1950s, song lyrics have become simply words, which don't matter because we don't think about them. We're not listening to the lyrics. How else could there be verse about a cake being left in the rain?

At least, being 1968 America, it rhymed. No wonder the songs became louder.

Late one night in the summer of 1991, my English travelling companion Deborah and I stood looking over the city of Cluj-Napoca. Ceaușescu had been overthrown but capitalist democracy had not yet taken root in Romania. Cafés sold Turkish beer I assumed had, figuratively speaking, fallen from trucks on route to Western Europe. Signs promoted American colas, although we couldn't find them for sale. Television sets played garish sounds and bright images from Music Television, M.T.V.: emotion without meaning, feelings without relationship, but also bold and brassy where nothing else was. The music in motion reeked of richness, if only in money: the bulwark for the coming new order.

Repetitive thumping thuds are African aggression, but that's what we want. Radio and television stations play music energising us to compete. We hear noise without music, rhyme without poetry: barely discernible words we can't decipher. Loud music saves us from conversation, leaving us comfortably compliant and alone. Thinking is intellect, but no one can think. Talking is relationship, but no one can talk. The solitary fool fares no worse than the wise with family and friends.

Supermarket and other store sounds push us through our most immediate commercial activity. Heavy, pulsating beats like racing hearts pump us like addicts hungry for drugs towards our next purchases. If melodious music and soulful song have their place, it's carefully chosen. Subliminal soft music draws us to buy bamboo fans.

We don't appreciate any music as much as we appreciate electronic sound systems. Tiny speakers tucked into corners of kitchens, bedrooms, bathrooms, even cupboards, play the music to relax or arouse. The swimming pool with the house that we bought appears to have provided for the connection of speakers underwater. Thankfully, no one installed them.

Our favourite entertainers became those not necessarily the most talented, but the ones we're accustomed to seeing or hearing. They became those with the best publicists.

We don't need fine arts anymore. We have celebrities. I couldn't name any song Lady Gaga has sung, even after my second daughter attended her concert, but I know of her dress sense and nudity.

Among the many careers available to aspiring consumers in our vacuous West, one is simply being famous. The celebrity is famous for no other reason: the marketing of self over substance, a person purely as image. A celebrity's talent for doing anything matters less than a publicist's talent for promotion. Being a rich, beautiful, young heiress without inhibitions or boundaries can help.

Notoriety needn't be privacy's loss. An image with stories to tell can be confined to the peripheries of a performer's life, or be contrived. The most publicised name around doesn't need to confess anything about the person behind. It's probably better if it doesn't.

Performers' personal lives are more entertainment, particularly when they're spiralling downwards. Intrinsically individualistic egos can be brittle great beasts, depending upon fame and the adoration of strangers. Photographers and journalists torment troubled stars because, somewhere along a line beyond magazine editors and television programmers, voyeurs pay money to watch. Entertainment is news and news entertainment. The unravelling of American singer Britney Spears' young life sold so many magazines and employed so many people, I once heard her described as an industrial complex.

The definitive great composer Ludwig van Beethoven was German, but we're doggedly determined not to own anything good. Sometimes bandied about is the claim Beethoven was black, as a white woman told me was self-evident from the most famous engraving of him, but all engravings are black on cream or white paper. Jamaican writer Joel Augustus Rogers claimed all manner of historical figures, including several popes, monarchs, and American presidents, carried at least a drop of African blood in their veins. No reputable scientific authority shares his view.

If we really thought Beethoven was black, we might again listen to his Pastoral Symphony and other orchestral melodies. Young Germans might appreciate them. We don't listen to our musical heritage, because it's our own.

What Ian Plimer on that 2010 mining industry cruise credited to Christianity I'd never before appreciated is our musical tradition. Europe and God inspired our classical composers, much as they inspired our painters and sculptors. It might also have inspired Reuben, or inspired singers among the choirs performing evensong at our parish Anglican church.

Each term of my schooling at Knox Grammar Preparatory School from 1969 began and ended with full school assemblies, at which we sang hymns dedicated to the opening and closing of terms. At morning assemblies throughout the year, we sang hymns like 'Onward Christian Soldiers,' without thought of war but confidence, conviction, and togetherness. We might've done the same at senior school; I can't recall.

No other religion offers such melody as our Christmas carols: the tenderness of 'Away in a Manger,' the glory of 'Hark the Herald Angels Sing.' During his atheistic or agnostic phase of life,

Englishman C.S. Lewis could not help but appreciate the sound of church music.

No sound is more stirring than a congregation singing old hymns, nothing more rousing than 'When I Survey the Wondrous Cross,' nor more touching than 'Amazing Grace.' Singing 'Abide with Me' in our parish Anglican church on Remembrance Day 2014 made Golden Cross Resources Limited, at which I worked at the time (but for only another month), easier to face. We sing and hear hymns in glorious adulation of God with our peoples. Needless to say, Plimer isn't amongst us.

For the most part, we who stirred in times of yore to sing 'How Great Thou Art' no longer sing. We no longer stir. The Psalms offer every human emotion, but we only want happiness.

No longer basking in Bach, Johann Sebastian, our postmodern church music became much like the rest of our music: banal monotonous lines about each individual us. They might speak to our devotion, but they're about us. We repeat them over and over.

Without us asserting our religion, the music around us resounds no longer with our Christian faith but with hostility towards it. Bisexual black Trinidadian singer Nicki Minaj appeared on stage at the 2012 American Grammy music awards with stained glass behind her and a man dressed as the Pope, in a show that included faux monks, choirboys, holy water, a confessional, levitation, demonic possessions, and an exorcism. A scantily clad female dancer stretched backwards, while an altar boy knelt between her legs in prayer.

"Never would they allow an artist to insult Judaism or Islam," pointed out Catholic League president Bill Donohue. Minaj would say she was Christian.

The *National Names Database*, which referred me to the story, commented not upon Minaj but upon the Christians. "*Easily offended people complain about Nicki Minaj.*"

Never have I seen people complaining about Christianity or even just Christmas so derisorily mocked. We don't mock people of other races easily feeling offence.

The best, perhaps only, known musical instruments of the Australian Aborigines are long, thin, hollow trunks of wood called didgeridoos. Their bellowing roars are synonymous with red Australian deserts at sunset and campfires plying into the night, although I suspect most corroborees still performed are shows for schoolchildren and tourists. The *Daring Book for Girls* in 2008 instructed readers (presuming the book's readers to be girls) on blowing a didgeridoo, never imagining it was a male instrument. (With hindsight, it seems obvious.)

The controversy was quick. Indigenous commentators compared allowing girls to play the didgeridoo with letting people play with razor blades.

We chastise each other for sexism but respect Aboriginal sexism; conflicting values between colonial Europe and indigenous races are the conflicts so central to our multiculturalism. The publisher apologised if it had inadvertently offended anyone. Nobody mocked Aborigines for being easily offended.

If racial diversity and multiculturalism created anything worthwhile, and I'm not sure they have, then it's if Africans believe they couldn't have sung the blues in Lesotho they sing in Louisiana. They don't need London for that.

Few church services I've seen were more enjoyable than one I observed for African Americans in a Harlem church, late in the 1990s. We were tourists watching the show from a gallery: visitors, for a mere portion of the service. The music was theirs. (The church had become theirs.)

When our minds turn to our culture, it's estranged from our people. France mandated that French radio stations play forty percent of music in French from the beginning of 1996, but French musicians sang in English. The law advanced immigrant musicians playing black American hip-hop and rap, albeit in French, including Monsieur R's 'FranSSe' attacking France for her treatment of immigrants.

Our dance is no less African than our music. We no longer waltz, nor promenade, nor work a ballroom with European grace. We've become anarchy, bouncing around in dark nightclubs. We're individuals: men and women no longer touching, barely able to recognise each other. We dance like we live, but to music.

17. PROSE AND POETRY

Around the eighth or seventh century Before Christ, Greek poet Homer reputedly crafted his epic poem the *Odyssey*. Its solitary hero overcoming great perils through his ten-year journey home after war put individual acts and personal quests at the forefront of Western thinking.

Our individual acts and personal quests were in the context of our families and peoples. We have lost our families and peoples.

"*The mass of men lead lives of quiet desperation*," wrote Henry David Thoreau in his 1854 non-fiction book *Walden*. He might've been right about America in 1854. I'm not sure he still is, of the West.

My accounting colleague Fred spent a year in England, working on a new catamaran ferry service for Holyman Limited. When he wasn't working, Fred was in his hotel room or the house the company rented. Not me. After we'd spent Saturday working through the launch of the new service, I led Fred to Canterbury for the night and Sunday, inspecting the cathedral and the *Canterbury Tales* visitors centre. From one of Chaucer's fourteenth-century tales, I learnt that a woman above all else wants sovereignty. That hasn't changed.

For all Kim's rejection of his British heritage, he appreciated Western literature, as I learnt after I mentioned to him my first novels. He read one, and concluded with the advice I should buy, read, and write like anything by Canadian novelist Robertson Davies.

Among the idealistic, young soldiers initially setting off to the Great War were those imagining war to be ennobling, in a world they thought required it. In his poem 'Peace', British poet Rupert Brooke described them "*as swimmers into cleanness leaping, Glad from a world grown cold and old and weary.*" Brooke died in the first year of the war.

Born in French Algeria to a poor French farmworker who died in the Great War and a half-deaf Spanish woman, Albert Camus expressed better than anyone else our disconnect from our people, families, and selves amidst a second world war. His opening words of his novel *The Stranger* or *The Outsider* (*L'Étranger*), first published in 1942 could have been mine, after my mother died.

Among the books I studied at school was half-Jewish American J.D. Salinger's *The Catcher in the Rye*, published in 1951. It was young white America, listless and lost, without confidence in her past or elders.

Half a century later, we'd rather write, or type, than read. Never before have so many written as much as we write today. Never before has so little of it been worth reading.

We use literature for the same reasons we use everything else: advancing our globalist vision at the expense of our countries and cultures. The slogan for the 2011 Children's Book Council of Australia Book Week (everything had a slogan by 2011) was "*One World, Many Stories,*" blaring from every noticeboard placed conspicuously outside every primary school I saw. Scholastic book publishers provided the poster affixed to the Wahroonga Preparatory School library window, in which Robin Hood was at least some reference to England. From the Middle East, of equal importance in the poster, was Aladdin. From Australia, was a story of Aborigines.

All the peoples on earth want their children (and some also want our children) to read literature conveying their viewpoints. Our postmodern literature abrogates all other considerations.

We're no longer teaching great literature with messages we endorse. We're just teaching the messages, and the messages are political. Any rubbish saying the right things will do.

Captive in class, the first book my youngest son's year-four teacher told the children to read was Jewish writer Morris Gleitzman's fictitious *Boy Overboard*. The story of Asian refugees coming to Australia convinced the boys and girls those Asians were brave. Wanting to join the Australian soccer team made them seem like us.

Henry Handel Richardson is out of the picture. Not a single course in the country still asks students to read her classic novel *The Fortunes of Richard Mahony*. I'd never heard of it.

Well-written stories, well-performed songs, and well-made films by people skilled in persuasion ought to fare better than anything mediocre to convince people the truth of the truth, although it doesn't always seem so. It's nigh on impossible for writers with whom we disagree, or with whom the people who set school syllabuses disagree, to be heard. A voice isn't a voice if no one can hear. Publishers don't care what people happen to think if they're not buying books. They don't always care if they are.

If we're not picking messages we already believe, we don't want messages at all. "I read books for pleasure," said the programme director of a Melbourne radio station, "not to read about the problems of the world." (I can't see him reading my non-fiction books.) Clarke didn't want, in respect of the first novels I wrote, what inanely I called human truths.

It's hard getting books published when publishers don't understand what writers are trying to do. It's even harder when they do understand. Censors once banned books for offending sexual mores. Today they're banned for offending ideologies. The only literature now worth writing is offensive.

We want books to entertain us with words that don't matter: words without meaning. Whatever the objectives behind them, books compete with other entertainment.

Our literature is nuanced. "If your book's about what your book's about," said Roland Fishman of the Writers' Studio in Bronte, "then you're in trouble." Whether he meant that to apply to non-fiction, I hope I'm not in trouble.

In the business of literature, money comes from transactions: books purchased and sold. Shelly's Bookshop didn't convene our philosophy club to discuss philosophy but to buy books, observed another lawyer John much afterwards. We couldn't consume a book each meeting and so couldn't buy a book each meeting. Sales slowed, the bookshop closed, and after a few meetings in Pablo and Rusty's coffee shop, the philosophy club withered and ceased.

Being impatient, the first phrase of a book had better seize our attention. We might buy it and not read any more, but that doesn't matter. We've already bought. Each page that absorbs us into escape encourages us onward. If the ending is happy enough, then we liked it. We'll tell others to buy it.

For people unable to last more than a few minutes without eating or drinking, stores contain coffee shops. Another trend I first encountered in America eagerly adopted elsewhere was for bookstores to become cafeterias. We wile away time with beverage and books, without troublesome conversation or company.

Without expertise, consumers have familiarity. We might read a writer, or genre, in which we've enjoyed past experience. Famous writers need only their names on the cover to sell their next works; the better known the writer, the bigger the font for his or her name.

The success of one genre, of magic and wizards, inspires mimicry as does the success of any other product or service, until people grow weary. *"Nothing succeeds like excess,"* wrote Irishman Oscar Wilde, in his 1893 play *A Woman of No Importance*. Most writers have little time to experiment with anything new, any more than do consumers.

Literature is a service, not a good: transient and abandoned. When Roly gave me a Tom Clancy book to read, I thought he was being kind, until I saw the book was embossed with a Qantas airlines sticker. He had taken it from a flight.

We no more have libraries of books in our homes than our offices. (I have a library at home, but time to read little. I hope someday to read every book there.) When that radio station programmer Clarke finished reading a book, he gave or threw it away. Electronic books we needn't notice deleting or not.

The books we don't discard are decorative adornments. Instead of pictures around some law office walls stand libraries of court reports, long after computer files and sites made bound reports superfluous. (Law isn't easy to picture.) The Sydney meeting room for the Walford Partnership recruitment firm in 2006 housed a bookshelf of leather-bound editions in several different languages, collected by one in the firm.

Never too many, but the occasional book at one end of a shelf, between shining clean bookends or beside a ceramic round vase, can make the most moronic of people seem erudite. Impressing visitors with the breadth of our interests, we made English physicist Stephen Hawking a bestselling writer, although few people read much of *A Brief History of Time* or learnt anything about cosmology or mathematics. The black holes most affecting consumers are the ones from our credit cards.

Executives and ambitious employees buy books concerned with our work, especially those that compliment people we know or companies for which we've worked. Autobiographies by people still in their careers tend to be self-promoting. Those by people retired from their careers tend to be self-justifying. If we never read them, the books sit on our office shelves so people think we have read them. If we have read them, we hide them at home so people don't know that we have.

Dulling language is easy with plagiarism, which lawyers call precedent. Our compositions avoid anything personal.

Business language focuses upon the task at hand, without distractions of emotion or colour. It would be interesting to imagine what commercial documents might be like if somebody wrote them as literature, describing characters with personalities. In the minutes of meetings, the chairman might flinch. The chief executive might turn his head away, thinking about the young woman temporarily assigned to the reception desk (as often appeared the case at Cement Australia). A director's gaze might become lost in the grains of wood veneer on the table.

The minutes might've mentioned the point in one meeting when the eyes of the chairman of that shipping company at which I worked slowly closed. Other directors let Dick rest, carefully not addressing anything to him. Perhaps they prolonged the discussion to give him time to wake, or another director deftly guided the meeting without him. Dick woke, without comment by anyone on his slumber or reference to it in the minutes I drafted.

Words drafted as literature wouldn't survive their first executive review, let alone reach the chairman. Not only are company directors uninterested in frivolity, they're unwilling to seem different to other directors. Someone might laugh.

Something creative in our Western minds remains unsatisfied by our postmodern fixation with spending and work. For many of us, creativity's last expression is devising names for new companies and code names for projects. Union Shipping chief executive Ken Urry said the most difficult negotiations for any joint venture were normally those for the name.

We became less and less representative of our people, catering to multiculturalism, and less and less imaginative. The name of Cement Australia comprised its principal product and the country to which its shareholders confined it; I'd hate to think of a marketing consultant being paid for that one. At Golden Cross Resources Limited, Kim pointed out that the trend in company names was towards letters. We follow fads wherever we can.

At least we have nature. The secret plans to merge the companies that became Cement Australia in 2003 were known as Project Jacaranda, apparently because someone looked out an office window and saw jacaranda trees in bloom. One floral name chosen, the human resources department later named its targets to reduce numbers of employees: the sweet smelling Project Wattle. Never was firing people more aromatic.

The merger process had concluded with several initiatives intended to reduce business costs by a hundred million dollars a year: Project Omega. Few of us realise our classical Greek heritage.

Naming the new company internal computer site was the subject of a competition among employees. Launched with colourful cards and equipped with current technologies, the winning name was a woman's name Caz, in that most masculine of companies. It was also an acronym; we like acronyms. Competitions among staff came without prizes. Naming anything is its own reward.

The previous decade, in the secretive world of company boards and merchant banks plotting company takeovers, the vestiges of our literary tradition hovered. Another company refused to match the terms on which that shipping company for which I worked secured Belgian government endorsement for that new high speed English Channel ferry service. It then watched the shipping company founder. Before becoming the shipping company's joint venture partner in the service, it investigated acquiring its rival, using the code name Project Hesperus.

My knowledge of Longfellow's poem about a ship wrecked in a hurricane came from my mother describing me in my younger years of long hair, flannelette shirts, and denim jeans as "looking like the wreck of the Hesperus." In spite of the shipping company sinking towards insolvency when all of us employees would surely lose our jobs, the name Project Hesperus made me smile.

If prose struggles to survive in our commercial lives, poetry fares worse. If my book *Christendom Lost* sounds like Englishman John Milton's epic poem *Paradise Lost* exploring the Biblical story of the Fall of Man, then so it should.

Only after our return from a holiday did I notice the words of an old Australian poem on the front of a tourist brochure I'd picked up in Bathurst, striking me with the sense such poetry had become unknown in Sydney. Poetry becomes obsolete and all the poets die, before the world around them dies. Our postmodern poets save time without rhythm and rhyme; their blank verse is industry, hurried and bland, distinguishable from business memoranda only by the matters on which they muse and because no one pays them to write. People don't read it.

A black friend of my younger sister in London wanted the British government to pay him money other people earned to write poetry all day. I'd have preferred the government pay Leroy not to write. He might have too.

In his nineteenth-century poem 'The Charge of the Light Brigade,' Alfred, Lord Tennyson wrote of the most tragic of brave British soldiers. "*Theirs not to make reply, Theirs not to reason why, Theirs but to do and die.*"

In our postmodern West, we're not so brave but are much more tragic. Ours is not to reason why. Ours is but to do and buy.

18. FILMS

"The life history of the race repeats itself in each individual," teacher Miss Elsie Thornton told her class of graduating students in the 1957 American film *Peyton Place*.

The 2009 Australian television film *3 Acts of Murder* depicted real events, and captured as well as anything now could our malaise when the soldiers came home from the Great War. Murder was almost by the by, because death had been promiscuous.

We recovered, to a point. Until I told my six-year-old youngest daughter I would buy a copy of the 1937 American film *Snow White and the Seven Dwarfs* (from the then-great Walt Disney Studios and, at the time, the most successful film ever made), she'd never heard of it. (Speaking of dwarfs had become offensive in the West by the time she was born.)

Western children now see other people's shows but, animations aside, probably the most accessible reminders of what we were, with hints of what we could have become, are old films. If they seem to have dwelt too much on the best we could be, it's because we wanted to be the best we could be.

World War II jarred us into a deeper nihilism than had the Great War, ushering in the foreboding film noir. The West all became a bit German. Blonde women were *femmes fatales* because Nazi Germany so seductive proved so destructive.

We found consolation in races over which we'd previously felt superior. Only one character in the 1952 British film *Hunted* wasn't European. Dirk Bogarde (born Derek van den Bogaerde) played a murderer fleeing the law left destitute, who asked a well-groomed African passer-by on the street for a cigarette. The African cheerfully obliged, speaking with a voice upper class by comparison. He produced a fine cigarette case from which he generously insisted the vulnerable protagonist take his last cigarette. The African was nobler and kinder than we thought us to be.

We weren't so keen to hear bad things of other races. American writer Agnes Keith wrote of the brutal Japanese treatment of

Western men and women during World War II in her 1948 memoir *Three Came Home*, which became a film in 1950. "...*I find that one or two critics (not 'The New York Times') question why the story was written*," she wrote to the *New York Times* newspaper, in a letter published the last Sunday in March 1950.

As they'd done before World War II, actors and actresses became famous conveying characters that viewers found enticing: the laconic hero, sultry warrior, suave gentleman. After the first James Bond film *Dr. No.*, in 1962, all the villains in Bond films were white until *Live and Let Die* in 1973. Good black characters and bad white ones didn't free that film from accusations of racism for villains being black. The Chinese villain in *Flash Gordon* led to accusations that 1980 film perpetuated the stereotypical evil Oriental.

I can't overstate the impact of the horrible Holocaust on not just Jewish culture but Western culture, too. America's moral code restricting nudity in films began to break down because of the 1965 film *The Pawnbroker*, based upon a 1961 novel of that name by Jewish writer Edward Wallant. The story and characters in the film were fictitious, but censors relaxed their prior prohibitions. They subjected cinemagoers to fleeting images of a prostitute exposing her bare breasts to pawnbroker Sol Nazerman, because they invoked in his mind the trauma of the Holocaust. Those bare breasts reminded him of his wife's breasts, before Nazis raped her.

No longer were we catering to popular sensitivities. We were trying to change them. Seeing World War II through Jewish eyes, the Jewish view of our past prejudice became ours. We feel what Jews have felt since 1945. Their perspective of the world became ours.

Like other media, wide-release films reflect some of the values we hold, while promoting the values we will. Aliens had been threatening until the 1951 American film *The Day the Earth Stood Still*. That alien was wise and benevolent, while warmongering humans needed a lecture in peace. The alien proved his power not by action but inaction, shutting everything down. It might've been the first environmentalist film.

Our films have become no less ideological than the rest of our fine arts. The enemies they describe are us and our Western authorities, as they were to Jews through the Holocaust.

Viewers identify with the oppressed. An alien was the victim trying to flee the American government in the 1982 American film *E.T.: The Extra Terrestrial*.

In the 1984 film *Starman*, an alien without physical form took the form of a white American, demonstrating how much alike we are, at our best. (Never mind racial diversity.) While pointing out we'd invited aliens to come, the enemy it fled was the American military.

Another alien without physical form needed only to learn English in the 1989 film *The Abyss*. Its most dangerous foe was Lieutenant Hiram Coffey from the American Navy's Sea, Air, and Land Teams, usually abbreviated as SEALs.

The empathy we feel for other life forms, we feel for other races. We shouldn't be any less empathetic if they're not always peaceful. (We aren't.)

In 1982 came the futuristic *Blade Runner*. Human beings had developed clones to perform dangerous and degrading work on Earth's colonies, some of whom we utilised on Earth before a minor uprising led Earth's authorities to expel them. The title character tracked them down, before learning from them what being alive could mean. We don't learn about life from our forebears or from God, but from other beings and races (who we also once enslaved).

Increasingly through the years since its release, critics came to love *Blade Runner* for depicting Los Angeles with every race and language scrambling for survival. We can no longer imagine any other future: dark, cluttered, and bleak, but post-national and perhaps even post-racial, with everyone individuals on individual quests. If films don't prophesy the future, they dictate it.

More blatantly than the rest of our arts (because everything about films is more blatant than the rest of our arts), our films aren't trying to advance civilisation, at least not ours. The world we portray is often worse than reality, but inspires audiences who believe what they see to accept the West in decline. Reality is trying to catch up.

We don't glorify. We terrify. The best we can do is find new ways to shock.

By the second decade of the new millennium, our most prevalent film villains were zombies: the dead. With nothing to fear from other races or aliens, our compatriots who die in the first act try to kill us in the second. They're our past: our ancestors and parents. We can believe they'd be hostile to us, thinking they were hostile to other races. No guardian angels from seats beside God, they're monsters from hell's deep ravines. They're us, when we die.

Overarching it all are political objectives. Nothing is more important than eradicating white racism.

"You're a racist," Natalie Wright told policeman and her former husband Ray DeCarlo in the 2001 American film *The Stickup*, after he blamed becoming a criminal upon the greedy Indians' casino ruining the Californian townspeople and bringing drugs to the high school. "That's worse than a thief."

In the 2008 American film *Gran Torino*, redemption for a racist white American wasn't just accepting the growing Asian population around him. It was saving one of them, even after the Korean tried to steal his car.

True stories can be no less fictitious than fictional ones, when the objective is avoiding white people's racism. The 1988 American film *The Accused* depicted the real-life rape of a young woman in a Massachusetts bar in 1983 and its aftermath. For all the filmmakers' efforts to make the rest of the film accord with the woman's ordeal that night and at the rapists' trial, they made the rapists and other defendants (as well as the victim) ordinary, homegrown Anglo Americans. In fact, the four rapists and people cheering them along at Big Dan's Bar in New Bedford that first Sunday night in March 1983, swapping turns to rape Cheryl Araujo, were immigrants.

Confronting audiences about the trauma of gang rape didn't warrant prejudicing audience's impressions of immigrants, even Portuguese ones, less we cease welcoming all comers. The real-life necessity for interpreters to translate the accused men's testimonies to English would have slowed the pace of the film, but the film could have portrayed them as Portuguese able to speak English. The victim was American Portuguese.

Race features prominently when we're complaining about white people's racism. The racism doesn't need to be real.

Soon after two thirty the penultimate Friday morning in June 1966, a black man murdered a white bartender and two white customers in a Paterson, New Jersey bar and grill, before walking out of the bar laughing. The bartender Jim Oliver and male customer Fred "Cedar Grove Bob" Nauyoks died immediately. The badly wounded female customer, Hazel Tanis, died almost a month later. A third white customer, Willie Marins, was shot in the head and lost sight in one eye. Courts twice convicted boxing champion Rubin "Hurricane" Carter of the crimes.

Film-makers initially claimed to be telling the true story of Carter with the film *The Hurricane* in 1999, but fictionalised much in their determination to portray him as an innocent victim of white racism. In real life, he lost a boxing match to a white American opponent Carmine Orlando Tilelli, known professionally as Joey Giardello, but the film falsely portrayed Carter winning in the ring only to lose because the judges were white racists. Tilelli sued the film-makers for damages, receiving money in settlement of his claim.

While including some of Carter's prison time, the film omitted a four-year term he served for assaulting three people. In that case, the investigating detective was black.

More telling than the omissions were the lies. The racist white detective Della Pesca investigating the bar and grill murders in the film was a complete fabrication. The film's producers called him a "composite character" of the allegedly racist attitudes of white New Jersey policemen at the time. What a world could be construed from composite characters?

In the make-believe film, the two juries convicting Carter of murder were all white. In reality, two black jurors sat on the second jury. In interviews, and in speeches he made to college campuses eagerly believing white racists imprisoned black heroes, Carter dismissed their verdicts because they were elderly. By the time I bought a copy of the film, the disc's covering case said it was merely "*based on the inspirational true story of a champion.*"

We believe that promoting racial tolerance warrants our deceptions, but deceptions they are. We dread telling the truth. Put another way, we espouse anti-racism themes.

For all the fine books and films condemning white people for our supposed prejudices against others, I've never seen any speak of other people being prejudiced against us. That would be racist.

Australian critic Peter Thompson described the 2001 American film *What's Cooking* as a "film that rejoices in the diversity of American life…a multiracial, multicultural, if not chaotic, atmosphere." He also made a rare admission that chaos and conflict arises from multiracialism and multiculturalism, although in the context of applauding them. "One frequently noted consequence of racial and cultural mixing is an explosion of creative energy. It can boil over into conflict, of course, and often does, but it also produces wonderfully exciting and unpredictable results."

Films to watch and review warrant the conflict, he felt. Without race to define us, artists (and critics) become defined not so much by their art as their disinterest in anything else.

Creative energy doesn't require racial diversity; India produces more cinematic films than any other country. Nor does energy equate to quality, although our convictions of equality prevent us from seeing the rubbish so much creative energy produces. We alone find racial and cultural diversity exciting because we no longer find our people exciting, in spite of all the arts and sciences, sports and culture, we achieved in our homogenous past. We never ran out of ideas as Hollywood has come to do, remaking old films for audiences who refuse to watch old films.

Writing became lazy, contriving conflict with cursing and cussing rather than character and predicaments. I've never heard anyone say he or she watched a film for the sake of the swearing but, sitting with me on a long drive to Molong in 2014, Kerry told me not to bother seeing *The Grand Budapest Hotel*. I didn't, but it was already a rare film I'd intended to see because of the poster that I decided not to see because of the trailer. For all the swearing some people make, none can rival second-rate characters in third-rate film scripts, or even otherwise first-rate characters in first-rate scripts.

When we tell stories to entertain, Western storytelling treasures the hero with flaws and the villain with virtues (except when they're racists). Only Jesus was perfectly good. Other races (except Jews) expect their heroes to be perfectly good and villains perfectly evil.

Jews are more complex. In talking about the 1989 film *When Harry Met Sally...*, Jewish screenwriter Nora Ephron distinguished the Christian tradition of romantic comedy from the Jewish. In the Christian, she said the obstacle keeping the man and woman from coming together is something external to them. In the Jewish, it's the man's neuroses.

Islam's core is the struggle of jihad. It leaves little room for romantic comedy.

The contrast between what was Western adventure and what remains Jewish angst was never plainer than in the 1986 musical

Into the Woods, which became a 2014 film. German brothers Jacob and Wilhelm Grimm's fairy tales could be scary, but the witches, wolves, and other dangers were external to the central characters inwardly comfortable with themselves and endings were happy. Jewish lyricist Stephen Sondheim and Jewish writer James Lapine added turmoil and tragedy afterwards.

The film felt like two films joined together because it was, much like the West trying to join Europeans and Jews together since 1945. Stark differences remain.

Rudyard Kipling's 1894 collection of stories *The Jungle Book* was the basis of the 2016 film of that name. "The strength of the wolf is the pack, the strength of the pack is the wolf," is a theme of the film, marrying the forces of nationalism with individualism, as the West in our glory days did. Mowgli learns that his survival depends upon him being what he is, rather than trying to be what he's not.

If few white Christians feel ownership of Christian Western culture or long to experience the cultural facets of faith, then white people with little interest in God or salvation are unlikely to do so, except that some do. American film-maker Emilio Estevez tactfully told Father Dave Dwyer's radio show in Los Angeles that his faith was "work in progress" in 2010, but explored the Christian tradition of pilgrimage in his film *The Way*.

His father Martin Sheen's faith was doubtlessly a reminder of his Roman Catholic heritage, although the fanciful sequence in the film promoting tolerance of gypsies depended upon a lack of family loyalty at home among Europeans more than among gypsies. (The 1996 film adaptation of Jane Austen's novel *Emma* more accurately represented gypsies.) Estranged from all sense of reality, another Resurrection at that point in *The Way* would've been easier to believe.

19. TELEVISION

Holed up in our homes, already alone, idle television and computer screens play floating images of space, wet rainforests, and imaginary bubbles. When we want entertainment, we turn towards them. Our heads are busts below spotlights, faces flickering against rectangles of light from glass and metal capsules or translucent plastic sheets. Computer keyboards and microphones converse through air and modem lines with other silhouettes. We play new versions of old games, with electric friends and enemies. Heavy rain could fall outside, but people transfixed by imagery don't see water streaming down their windows.

Secure in our homes, we prefer watching television to attending the cinema for the privacy, and for the ease of looking away when our concentration stalls. Television is cinema with an exit strategy.

We might not care what rubbish is broadcast through our television sets and computer screens, provided it comes in high definition. If we care, anything coming through our television set had better carry us away within the first few minutes, or we'll abandon it. Not content with complaining there's nothing to watch on free television, we subscribe to pay television. We still complain there's nothing to watch, save only for sport.

The screens bring sound and movement, without the intrusion of real human beings. They're activity in the lounge room, bedroom, and sometimes even refrigerator door in the kitchen: noise and presence giving each solitary person some semblance of company. They're background nobody needs notice, not forcing us to think. The television series *Police Squad!* "was cancelled because the viewer had to watch it in order to appreciate it," said American Broadcasting Company television executive Tony Thomopoulos in 1982.

Other American television comedy isn't so good. It requires canned laughter to alert the audience to the jokes.

Some of the best writing of late, and the most influential, has been for television. Better than a book, we can comfortably experience a programme or film without effort, relying upon other people's imagination without any of our own. We watch new versions of old programmes we don't realise we've seen, by subscription or hired for viewing at home. We don't keep libraries of films and television series any more than we keep them of books; discs bought are easily discarded. If any colourful documentary happens surreptitiously to teach us something, then it's not what we need to know.

Like other consumption, television can be human experience. In fairyland can be relationships, lingering the joys and terror, pains and love, we don't feel in the rest of our lives. Preferring happy lies to miserable facts or crying for characters unreal, we want comfort and consolation when actuality hurts. In fantasy are none of the complications reality can be.

We don't readily delineate actors and actress' performances from the rest of their lives. (Sometimes, it seems neither do they.) In the 1960s, strangers abused actor Barry Morse because his character in the American television series *The Fugitive*, a police lieutenant, was trying every week to apprehend a man he thought guilty of murder. The audience watching, but not Morse's character, knew the fugitive to be innocent.

Our best friends are fictional characters in television series and serials for their repetition, returning each day or week we're not otherwise engaged. They're artificial friends, pretend-people in pixels like those in print, whose hopes and fears, likes and dislikes we know better than we know anyone real. Lively talking and laughing, they demand nothing of us, while our thoughts are with the meeting at eight o'clock in the morning or the black cast-iron table advertised in the last commercial break. Without angst upon anyone, our times together end when we press the buttons on our remote control handsets.

The American science fiction television series *Star Trek* ran for three years from 1966. "*Star Trek* was an attempt to say that humanity will reach maturity and wisdom on the day that it begins not just to tolerate, but take a special delight in differences in ideas and differences in life forms," said creator Gene Roddenberry. Our vision post Holocaust moved from merely tolerating diversity to enjoying it, although I suspect Roddenberry only had certain ideas in mind: not those disagreeing with him. "If we cannot learn to actually enjoy those small differences, to take a positive delight in those small differences between our own kind, here on this planet, then we do not deserve to go out into space and meet the diversity that is almost certainly out there."

Jewish actors William Shatner and Leonard Nimoy and black actress Nichelle Nichols (with whom Roddenberry carried on an adulterous affair) playing Captain Kirk, Vulcan science officer Spock, and Lieutenant Uhura were the most obvious expressions of Roddenberry's thematic objectives. They weren't the only ones. There was something comical about every miscellaneous group of three co-operative crew members comprising a European, an African, and an Asian.

Half a century onwards, *Star Trek* films remain our most optimistic vision of the future. It's a universe in which races and species work and mate together, but without visible religion or other culture, aside from eating and drinking.

Ours are the generations shaped by television. Modern-era missionaries won't save the West by knocking on doors of people reading books or watching television sets alone, but by producing what they read and watch.

Paragraph 9 of a 2012 lawsuit filed in Tennessee by black Americans Nathaniel Claybrooks and Christopher Johnson noted that *"studies show that images presented in the media play a substantial role in the formation of people's racial attitudes and opinions."* People of colour were highly represented on American television programmes such as *Dancing with the Stars*, but dancing together is one thing. Romance is something else entirely.

Single men and women won the chance to become romantically involved with each other in *The Bachelor* and *The Bachelorette*. Claybrooks and Johnson alleged the producers of those programmes discriminated by not selecting them as contestants, in violation of Californian law and the 1866 Civil Rights Act (following the American Civil War) that barred businesses from refusing to contract with others because of their race. Paragraph 68 of their suit alleged that *"by only hiring white applicants, Defendants are making the calculation that minorities in lead roles and interracial dating is unappealing to the shows' audience. The refusal to hire minority applicants is a conscious attempt to minimize the risk of alienating their majority-white viewership and the advertisers targeting that viewership."*

The plaintiffs sought, unsuccessfully, a federal court order that the producers consider people of colour as finalists. *"With such a massive viewership,*" they alleged at paragraph 78, "*Defendants have the opportunity to help normalise minority and interracial relationships by showcasing them to mainstream America on The Bachelor and The Bachelorette.*"

The Australian version of *The Bachelor* in 2014 promoted interracial relationships with African American bachelor Blake Garvey, but critics complained too many of the women were white. Those women included Sam Frost, to whom Garvey proposed marriage in the final episode and quickly thereafter dumped to be with another contestant. (Racial homogeneity was looking pretty attractive.)

In the 1960s, witches and weirdoes in American series like *Bewitched*, *The Addams Family*, and a little less engagingly *The Munsters* could've been freaky but were friendly, family people. (If ever there was a television series that could have managed another actor taking a role, *Bewitched* was it. Couldn't Agnes Moorehead's Endora have set a spell upon the affable Dick York version and people who knew him, so they'd not notice him becoming irksome Dick Sargent?)

From 1963, Uncle Martin in *My Favourite Martian* was a nice, clever alien like those in films. The aliens Mork in *Mork & Mindy* from 1978 and Alf in *Alf* from 1986 were funny, too.

Rare aliens appearing benevolent but revealing themselves to be malevolent were the Visitors in the 1980s American television series *V*. Looking back twenty-five years afterwards, the series could have been a metaphor condemning immigration. At the time, without any subtlety, the metaphor condemned racial and religious prejudice. Inspired by Sinclair Lewis' 1935 novel *It Can't Happen Here* about a fascist dictator arising in America, writer Kenneth Johnson, born in 1942, created charismatic Visitor aliens promising to better the Earth, who were really lizard-like creatures determined to subjugate humans.

Scientists wrongly accused by the Visitors of treachery were, in our post-Holocaust eyes, like the Jews of the past. Characters in *V* repeated the point several times over, in case anyone missed it.

It's been many years since racist film or television characters haven't been obviously loathsome, or revealed to be loathsome, but there was a time, when campaigns against white racism were getting under way, that television programmes like *Love Thy Neighbour* running from 1972 (which became a stage play I saw performed in

Sydney) portrayed racist white people like Eddie Booth as humorous buffoons. Other white characters and sophisticated black characters had little trouble overcoming them. Those racists weren't contemplating physical violence against anyone, let alone establishing extermination camps, but they held poor opinions about black people or didn't want them living nearby. We the audience laughed at them, not with them.

They were working class. With our divisions by wealth and occupation, middle-class and rich racists would've been threatening. Working-class racists were stupid and funny. Little wonder we came to agree. We want to be rich.

By the 1980s, rich white characters in American television series like *Dynasty* didn't need to be racist to be appalling. They were unrelentingly awful in spite, or perhaps because, of their good looks, fine clothes, and mansions. Black American singer and actress Diahann Carroll saw her opportunity. She telephoned the programme's producer and, in her words many years later, "told him that he definitely needed me. I thought it would be very wise to be the first black bitch on television, and to do it properly, not to hedge it. Make sure she was really not likeable, but quite lovely."

Carroll created the role of Dominique Deveraux, formerly Lloyd, born Millie Cox. It was a great step forward for racial equality.

Children's home environments can be difficult to mould, except through television. Late in the 1990s, the manager of a New York Harbour ferry business with whom I worked enthused for the animated children's television series *Arthur*. Tom liked it for dealing with meaningful issues, teaching children something worthwhile. A dozen years later, my children described the show to me. The white character was an idiot, the coloured one a genius, and one episode treated adopting an Asian baby as so normal as not to be noticed.

What we used to call indoctrination, we now call dealing with issues. We deal with only one side.

My baby sons particularly enjoyed watching the British, Canadian, and Australian animated children's television series *Brum*, in which a plucky little car outwitted dopey burglars and petty thieves before the kind good-natured policemen took them away; I feel like I saw every ten-minute episode. Preventing the children from adopting their parents' public perception of white policemen capturing black criminals, every actor I saw portraying a policeman in the show was black. Every actor I saw portraying a criminal was white. That must have been life in Big Town.

We mock our old books and films for their racial stereotypes grounded in the reality of their eras. We've created new stereotypes at odds with reality.

If film and television villains are foreigners, they're more often than not the same foreigners they've been since the Second World War. They're Germans, Russians, or Serbs.

My children, especially my youngest son when he was six years old, loved the Canadian television series *Monster Warriors*, in which a group of children tirelessly and cleverly saved Capital City from a mad and villainous old film director able to bring the monsters from his time-worn black-and-white films to life. The children were North American, without accents. The villain was Klaus Von Steinhauer, who thrust out his words with a thick German accent.

We're determined to avoid reinforcing negative stereotypes about other races. The safest course is to create positive stereotypes about them.

David was an Australian Chinese with whom I studied at law school and who studied business at the Macquarie Graduate School of Management at about the same time as I did, early in the 1990s. There, early in the new millennium, I came across him with a friend, an Australian Chinese actor, who complained that the only acting work he could get was playing a lawyer or doctor.

"What a great stereotype!" I told him. "I'd love that kind of stereotype!"

They laughed. Little wonder that Asians now flock into medical and law schools. Other stereotypes we create haven't proved self-fulfilling.

We allow negative stereotypes about us. No longer are we supposed to assume nothing about the races of criminals. In spite of our experiences and those of people we know, we're supposed to assume criminals are white before imagining they're anything else. Trusting Western popular culture, we needn't fret about other races.

The devolution in our sense of ourselves (and in the messages we're trying to impart) through the last decades of the twentieth century and first decades of the twenty-first were very well evidenced in one of my favourite television series as a child: *Doctor Who*. The regenerating Time Lord travelling time and space was from the planet Gallifrey, but still very English.

The 1975 story 'The Ark in Space' was set on a futuristic space station long after the Earth had died. Human colonists lay sleeping to survive their long journey to a new home. "Homo sapiens," marvelled the Doctor. "What an inventive, invincible species. It's only a few million years since they crawled up out of the mud and learned to walk. Puny, defenceless bipeds, they've survived flood, famine, and plague. They've survived cosmic wars and holocausts and now, here they are, out among the stars, waiting to begin a new life. Ready to out-sit eternity, they're indomitable."

A message from a lost civilisation implored the colonists to persevere. "You are the chosen survivors," said the messenger. "You have been entrusted with a sacred duty, to see that human knowledge, human culture, human love, and faith shall never perish from the universe. Guard what we have given you with all your strength."

The space station was infected with an alien bug, which laid its eggs in the sleeping humans. A medical officer asked coldly if one of the Doctor's friends was of value. "Of value?" replied the Doctor's other friend. "She's a human being like ourselves! What kind of question is that?"

Saving the human race instead of the bugs was speciesist of the Doctor, but that was 1975. "It may be irrational of me," he remarked, "but humans are quite my favourite species."

The 1977 story 'The Talons of Weng-Chiang' was banned in America and Canada for including Chinese villains, as stories with white and even alien villains weren't. Whenever the series' producers feared Britons becoming intolerant of immigrants, they'd wheel out the menacing, intolerant daleks.

Early in the twenty-first century, a new version of the Doctor appeared. Sexual norms had gone or would go; he kissed another man. His assistants were black, or involved with people who were. Not wanting to fuel fears about immigration, there were fewer alien invaders. Far from being one of many Time Lords, the Doctor had become the last of his race, but without despair for being so: the ultimate expression of Western individualism. He continued working, still trying to save others: the white man's terminal burden.

In the 2005 story 'The End of the World', the Earth reached its natural demise. Rich and powerful aliens watched entertained, while the environmentalist Doctor befriended a tree creature. The last human being was a horrible construct of cosmetic medicine, skin stretched from side to side and barely human at all, but plainly European. Human beings had become blights on the universe but white as they have to be, if we're not to be racist. Fundamentally, we don't like ourselves anymore.

Written by homosexual Russell Davies, that grotesque last human being betraying humanity's remnants was a woman. I stopped watching the new series, weary of the soullessness of it all.

20. CULTURAL REVISIONISM

William Shakespeare's plays are filled with imagination outrunning fact, skewing truth in our entertainment. Our popular impression of King Richard III, if we have one at all or even know who he was, is the one the Bard crafted: a villainous and deformed *"foul bunch-back'd toad."* Shakespeare falsified the appearance of the last in the line of kings preceding the House of Tudor to court the favour of Her Tudor Majesty Queen Elizabeth I. Hers was the applause he wanted.

Falsification continues. In 2009, Babatunde Adetomiwa Stafford became the second black actor to play Romeo in Shakespeare's play *Romeo and Juliet* at the reconstructed Globe Theatre in London.

In Shakespeare's play *As You Like It*, Hymen, the Greek god of marriage officiates over the concluding wedding scene. In the 2009 production by the Globe Theatre, Hymen was black.

We do not simply welcome immigrants. We make gods of them.

As storytelling doyen Robert McKee told an audience in Sydney in which I sat in 2004, Macbeth was the most complex and compelling character in literature with fifty different dimensions to his behaviour, which Shakespeare never felt a need to explain. English writer Agatha Christie never felt a need to cloud her crime sleuth Miss Marple with a past.

Following Jewish psychiatrist Sigmund Freud's theories of the impact past experiences continue to have upon people, postmodern Western writers haunt our characters with history. Decades after Christie's death, in the *Marple* Independent Television series from England supposedly based upon Christie's novels and set in the first half of the twentieth century, Miss Marple pined for her long-lost love: a Great War soldier.

It was a fascinating choice of backstory, saying much for World War I's continuing impact. If Christie didn't sense it for the women she knew or indeed for all Europe and her colonies through her lifetime, then somebody else writing for television almost a century after the war did.

Most deeply scarring us was the Jewish Holocaust. English satirical novelist Tom Sharpe was the son of a Unitarian minister who'd sympathised with fascism through the 1930s. "My father died in 1944," he said later, "and I saw the Belsen films and I discovered that Hitler was not the man that I'd been led to believe he was." British soldiers liberated the Bergen-Belsen concentration camp in Germany in April 1945. "My mind was blown by the horror of what had been happening."

Published in 1948, Englishman George Orwell's novel *1984* foreshadowed the dangers of Soviet communism, at a time that many in Europe (repulsed by the past) found communism appealing. The book introduced readers to Big Brother: the personification of a ruling totalitarian dictatorship watching all citizens through television screen cameras, while tirelessly espousing slogans to a populace too busy with its lives to question. "*Who controls the past controls the future,*" wrote Orwell. "*Who controls the present controls the past.*"

Orwell could have been describing our multicultural West, where histories are as malleable as everything else. Relativism means there's no reality now and never was. Subtler and gentler than any crudely overt dictatorship, Big Brother is more a Big Sibling.

An exhibition of books in the State Library of Victoria in October 2011 quoted Orwell's 1946 essay 'Why I Write.' "*When I sit down to write a book, I do not say to myself, 'I am going to produce a work of art'. I write it because there is some lie that I want to expose, some fact to which I want to draw attention, and my initial concern is to get a hearing.*"

I know the feeling. White people have all become Richard III.

The history my children are taught in school is a revision that began to appear after World War II, most obviously in the 1960s. History is no longer defined just by the victors, but by historians and film-makers.

Based upon a 1964 comic novel, the 1970 American film *Little Big Man* mixed facts with falsehoods to denigrate America's military and Christianity through the nineteenth-century Indian wars, thereby protesting twentieth-century American support for South Vietnam in the Vietnam War. Both were white imperialism.

The 2019 British film *1917* made great efforts to present the experience of trench warfare in World War I, but introduced black and Indian soldiers to multiracial units in the British Army that were negligible or non-existent in the war. The relatively small numbers of Africans and Indians who did enlist served in their own regiments or in colonial regiments, such as those in the British Indian Army.

Furthermore, in promoting the trust and confidence we are supposed to place in human authorities, the film portrayed our political and military authorities as caring for our British solders' lives. Our authorities did not.

The 2017 British film *Darkest Hour* included much fiction about the early part of World War II, including a fictional scene in a carriage on the London Underground in 1940 in which several people inspire Winston Churchill with British patriotism. Not only was a black man Marcus Peters treated by Churchill and everyone else as being as British as the best of them, he was the most educated and erudite among them.

American films like *Saving Private Ryan* in 1998 portray multiracial American military units that weren't the reality of World War II. In *Captain America: The First Avenger* in 2011, combatants from several races formed Captain America's elite. They advance the myth that the war defended racial diversity, instead of precipitating it. The African rap music playing through the end credits of *Saving Private Ryan* only added to that sense, although Channel 7 mate wisely broadcast the film without those credits and music when I watched it in 2013. The ending was more profound without them.

At least that Captain America was still white. In July 2015, Marvel comics announced Steve Rogers' retirement as Captain America and his replacement with black man Sam Wilson, formerly the Falcon. That October, the new black Captain America fought America's new enemy: white Americans trying to protect their country from illegal immigrants.

In 2017, the British television series *Victoria* portrayed Lord Alfred Paget and Edward Drummond conducting a homosexual affair. In fact, the two men probably never met each other. Paget married and had fourteen children. There is no evidence of Drummond having any homosexual encounters.

Other characters in the series treated their homosexual relationship as normal. In the 1840s, such relationships were rare. People encountering them would have been horrified.

The West having become convinced that our forebears shared our views of the world, when we learn of an old record of a person thinking otherwise, we are appalled. Unable to see that person's attitude as normal for his or her time (and still normal for the rest of the world) and whatever his or her achievements, we dismiss that person as we dismiss dissidents today.

He or she becomes another person whose arts and crafts are prohibited. His or hers is another name to strip from streets and buildings, another statue to be torn down.

The great actor John Wayne personified male Americanism in film. Soon after his death in 1979, the Orange County Airport in California was renamed in his honour; he had lived nearby. It was named for his acting, not for his views about anything.

Four decades later, a 1971 *Playboy* magazine interview resurfaced, in which Wayne supported white supremacy and spoke derogatively about African Americans, Native Americans, and films with homosexual characters. Calls to rename the John Wayne Airport and to remove his statue from it became louder and more numerous. Among the people that local state senator Tom Umberg, of German descent, wanted the airport renamed to honour was Tibor Rubin, a Holocaust survivor.

Historical revisionism is easiest when we write, or rewrite, the stories. Amidst our revision of history, we revise our cultural heritage. We rewrite our great literature, from a time in which we believed in ourselves into our time in which we don't, along its way to the screen.

In his 1912 novel *The Lost World*, Scottish author Sir Arthur Conan Doyle described American Indians stranding our heroes in the Amazonian jungle. In the British Broadcasting Corporation's 2001 television production, the villain was a lunatic, murderous, white priest.

The Paddington Bear books I read when I was young shared the joys and comforts of London family life with a bear from Darkest Peru. The 2014 film redefined the story of single bear immigration into a propaganda piece for mass human immigration, at least to London. Criminals were white. The villainess was the whitest of white, espousing loyalty to blood families instead of looking after foreigners. What had been a loving English family had become dysfunctional. When Mister Brown dismissed the bear's lies, he dismissed the lies of all immigrants.

Mister Brown's redemption lay in learning immigrants were honest, sharing his home with them, and defending them. The nice Brown family decided families weren't biological, but encompassed other species. Everyone was different, Paddington told his Aunt Lucy and thus the audience, dismissing any sense of Englishness in favour of multiculturalism and individualism. He thought that meant everyone could get along (however plainly people in reality don't).

Charles Dodgson, a mathematics tutor at Oxford University in the mid nineteenth century, published several mathematical and literary works. Under the pseudonym Lewis Carroll, he wrote *Alice's Adventures in Wonderland* and *Through the Looking-Glass*, which were loosely the bases for the 2010 American film *Alice in Wonderland*. Wearing two pairs of glasses, the first three-dimensional film I saw at a cinema only accentuated the one-dimensional milieu of the film.

The film's most memorable words came at the end, and couldn't have been more at odds with Carroll and his culture and stories. Not only did the emboldened heroine Alice turn down marriage and family in favour of a career, as our postmodern West tells women to do, she did so by rejecting the revolting English lord who wanted to marry her, while endorsing trade with China and what she called its "rich culture."

The irony of such messages, in the enduring final moments of the film, was inescapable, if only to me. Carroll's stories were features of England and English culture we value so little, while we value China and its culture. We're also fixated with commerce.

The film-makers might have been appealing to the huge Chinese market. Chinese people, along with most races on earth, like being told their culture is rich. We don't. It's inconceivable to describe any Western culture as rich, even when we're drawing upon it.

Yet in 1931, the governor of Hunan province in China banned *Alice's Adventures in Wonderland*. He felt animals shouldn't be raised to the same level as people.

In 1781, the crew of the British slave ship *Zong* threw more than a hundred and thirty Negro slaves overboard, after the ship became low on drinking water. The incident spurred the abolitionist movement in Britain ultimately ending slavery in the British Empire.

The 2013 nominally British film *Belle* portrayed African woman Dido Elizabeth Belle as developing the legal argument in the insurance court case. In reality, Belle had nothing to do with the case. The many historical inaccuracies in the film romanticised an illegitimate African woman in eighteenth-century Britain.

Much of what happens with films happens with television, but week after week, day after day. Englishman Daniel Defoe's classic 1719 novel *Robinson Crusoe* reflected our eighteenth-century vision of European empires civilising noble savages.

In 2008, the British, South African, and Canadian television series *Crusoe* portrayed our twenty-first century postmodern perspective. "He is my equal, my better in many ways, and my friend," white man Crusoe corrected the woman thinking black man Friday was his slave. Even calling the black man "Friday" became a joke on Crusoe's inability to pronounce his African name.

The producers of the British series *Downton Abbey* went to great lengths to be historically accurate in portraying an aristocratic Yorkshire family early in the twentieth century, with one sizable exception. For fear of alienating increasingly atheistic Britons, executives ordered the producers to "leave religion out of it," explained historical adviser Alistair Bruce. "We never see the beginning of a luncheon or a dinner, because no one was ever allowed to see a grace being said, and I would never allow them to sit down without having said grace." He couldn't even include napkins folded in the shape of a bishop's mitre.

Director of television Peter Fincham revealed that Independent Television had considered renaming the series. It was concerned about the title including reference to an abbey.

The 1992 television version of the Inspector Alleyn mystery *Death at the Bar* suggested a relationship between Norman and Sebastian. In the book upon which the programme was based, Norman proposed marriage to a woman, Decima.

The 2008 British Broadcasting Corporation production of *Appointment with Death* was part of the *Poirot* series, but with changes from Agatha Christie's novel upon which it was supposedly based. Most grotesque of all were those surrounding the addition of a Roman Catholic Polish nun. Not merely was she mad, but she commissioned an Arab slave trader to enslave a pretty European girl. (When Arabs do wrong, we're manipulating them.) Of any other race but European and any other religion but Christianity, that would've been bigotry. Of a Polish nun, it was entertainment.

The episode closed with Poirot telling the European girl of almighty god. The slander wasn't of all theistic religions, after all: just one.

Still, nothing I've watched has rivalled the *Marple* television series. Similarities were few between the television story *The Sittaford Mystery* and the Christie book of that name; even the murderer changed. A near-final scene in the television version, set soon after the Second World War, closed the story on two pretty, young Englishwomen. One was a recent widow. The other had twice been a young man's fiancée. Western stories are supposed to be about characters finding redemption, but these two confidently decided their future was together in Buenos Aires, "and it doesn't involve men."

Deviations from the book reached well beyond the literary and historical into the furthest reaches of fantasy. After that scene in the television story, although apparently not because of it, the murder victim returned from the dead.

A rare, perhaps only, character from a Christie novel who might have been homosexual was Mister Pye in *The Moving Finger*. Not content with hinting at a mere possibility, the television version made him flagrantly homosexual. In our revisionist history, homosexuals don't need to hide. Pye gave a passionate speech defending, even affirming, homosexuality to people around him, and thus the audience watching at home.

In the television version of the novel *By the Pricking of My Thumbs*, English villagers accepted without question what they thought were two women buying a cottage together, but the images we're advancing aren't just of happy homosexuals. They're also of miserable heterosexuals. A happily married woman in the novel became an alcoholic, bored housewife in the television version.

They're images of a failed church and religion. An unmarried vicar in the novel became an adulterous alcoholic seeing no meaning in life.

Wholly new to the television version was a heroic black American air force man, although very few American air force men at the time were black. (There didn't need to have been any for one to appear in our reconstruction of history.) The English village policeman planted false evidence that the black man committed a murder (as we insist happens all the time) because the pretty English girl loved him, but the girl's father and rest of those 1940s villagers embraced the multiracial couple. If heterosexuals were happy in our revisionist history, then they were in interracial relationships.

Commenting about the television production after its broadcast in 2006, readers of the original novel were careful not to complain about most of those changes. If they knew that portrayal of village England sixty years earlier was a fabrication, they said nothing about it. They complained only about the alcoholism.

It's an interesting new tact on simply lambasting our forebears for their prejudices. The racial and sexual diversity we've come to espouse in more recent years becomes part of our suddenly acceptable past. The failings of heterosexual marriage, Christianity, and white policemen become nothing new. The beauty of black men and white women loving each other becomes timeless.

The 2007 adaptation of *Ordeal by Innocence* didn't just add Miss Marple to a story without her. What had been a single English foster child became a series of interracial adoptions.

The first Sunday in July 2009, *Why Didn't They Ask Evans?* was at least simplistically similar to the book I recalled reading as a child. That said, the television writers added more murders and complicated stories around the victim's relatives. He'd long ago murdered his brother and married his dead brother's widow. She'd abandoned her crazy children by both marriages. Families had become the tortured and torturers, more wretched than mere murder had been in the novel.

The controversy over historical falsehood in fiction is an old one. Historical falsehood in what purports to be fact is relatively new.

The 2007 American, British, and Canadian television series *The Tudors*, portraying the court of King Henry VIII, included many historical inaccuracies that might have been inadvertent or for dramatic purposes. Giving the married courtier William Compton a homosexual relationship was complete fabrication.

Promoting racial and sexual diversity by presenting a falsified history in which they were normal and socially accepted in Europe does not please everyone. It undermines the competing narrative that we should compensate other races and homosexuals for having supposedly oppressed them throughout history. The historical reality, of immigrants and homosexuals being rare, does not suit either political objective.

Russell Davies wrote the 2005 British television series *Casanova* inspired, in the most obtuse way, by the classic memoirs of Giacomo Casanova, an Italian born in Venice in 1725. Set in the eighteenth century, the television series included a promotion for a single European currency and Casanova inventing a national lottery. His claim that the lottery led to the 1789 French Revolution was a call for revolution in 2005 Britain, with her national lottery.

In Davies' revisionist history, Africans shared the highest levels of Phoenician, French, and London societies, with everyone oblivious to race (which probably wasn't meant to be a reason for revolution). "I'm told the milk is terrible," Casanova said of England. "Oh, and a lot of the men are homosexual. That might have something to do with the milk, might not."

A character described homosexuality as blasphemy and a sin, almost as an aside, fobbing off not homosexuality but Christianity. At least Casanova remained heterosexual.

Near the end of the last episode, Casanova was in Naples. He refused to join his past conquest, the mixed-race Bellino, sniffing cocaine.

"The man who'll try anything," Bellino's daughter Leonilda chided her father, Casanova. "That's what you're famous for. That's your legend."

Leonilda and Casanova's son planned to sleep together, telling Casanova his life of sleeping with any woman anytime effectively espoused incest. Casanova was appalled, but ignored. He'd begun a path defying society and sexual moralities, but couldn't keep others from every illogical progression.

Mount Vesuvius erupting behind them reflected Europe's deep nihilism and fatalism, not in Casanova's time but ours. Death is inevitable and life beyond our control, thinks the West, however good or bad we are. At any moment, we could die, as so many of us died through two world wars. Many more could have died through the Cold War threatening thereafter and every danger since then. No less than the power we feel over all the races on earth, and even the Earth itself, is the sword of Damocles hanging above us.

There's no morality or sanction in the shadows of our demise, not anymore. Depraved, debauched, and doomed, dark days for

Europe are dark days for the world.

21. HAUTE COUTURE

Our theatre expressed the empty victory of World War II. Tennessee Williams' plays of the decline of the American South were the decline of white America.

In Britain, John Osborne's 1957 play (and 1960 film) *The Entertainer* was of Britain empty behind the eyes. The war songs Englishmen and women sang long afterwards exuded past happiness, from a time we'd bonded with optimism for what victory in World War II could mean. Singing them unconvincingly accentuated how little victory had brought. Not even the great Admiral Lord Nelson, shot and killed during his final victory at the Battle of Trafalgar in 1805, still mattered. When Archie Rice found hope in a fat Negress singing, he expressed a people finding comfort not in themselves but in others. "Why should I care?" he sang at the end.

Playing Rice was English actor Laurence Olivier, who sent Welsh actor Richard Burton a cable, saying: *"Make up your mind, dear heart. Do you want to be a great actor or a household word?"*

"Both," the ambitious Welshman replied. He wasn't acting. Great actors thrived on the stage, projecting their whispers. Lousy actors yelled. Household words were unlikely to rise from the theatre.

Half a century onward, during my time at Cement Australia, the eager communications manager referred to a "glass menagerie" amidst a telephone conversation with the business improvement manager. (I'm not sure how fragile were the people of that company, but we were certainly a menagerie and certainly isolated.) After that conversation concluded, Chloe suggested that only she and I among the twelve hundred employees would've understood her reference.

Chloe was probably the only other employee to understand my nickname for the embittered Sueki, whose surname returned from her English married name to its East Asian origins after her divorce. I called her "Madame Butterfly." (Sueki was Malaysian

Chinese rather than Japanese; I took a lot of operatic licence.)

Competing with cinema, theatre shows had become increasingly musical with spectacular special effects, while we keep from the stage anything challenging the greatness of everyone else or our self-disbelief. Amidst their globalist multiculturalism, Norwegians by 2011 wondered what role remained, if any, for their national figures like Henrik Ibsen. If Norwegians aren't teaching their children about their greatest playwright, whose home I was privileged to visit in Oslo, then nobody's teaching children about him.

Without us teaching our children our heroes and heroines, they'll never know. Prime Minister John Howard and education minister Brendan Nelson wanted Australian children to hear stories of Australians, such as Simpson and his donkey (or donkeys) during the Great War.

Our noble, naïve nations' confidence in their leaders proved to be misplaced when those leaders blundered into and through the 1914 war. Our governments and churches deserved to lose their diminishing authorities since then.

A century later, authority among European peoples remains with those few in whom others have confidence in their abilities and with whom they share collective interests. They might be military units if not military forces overall, the most successful sporting teams, or casts and crews making films and plays. The queens and kings to serve are those ruling with their people: nationalistic servants of the led.

They're hard to find. Before the two world wars, our elite saw themselves as the world's elite for being the elite of our races, countries, and Europe. Today, we're simply the world's self-supposed elite, feeling more in common with the best of other races than the ordinary of our own. Ours decline while others rise, but we imagine ourselves rising with others.

My friend James, a partner of a major accountancy firm, once agreed the only identity making sense for us was being British. Faithfully, he donned robes solemnly assisting the priest officiating services at our parish Anglican church. He was also a monarchist who led loyal toasts to Her Majesty after Queen's Birthday Evensong, but wasn't so loyal to his race. "*She talks about protecting her culture*," he wrote of Australian senator Jacqui Lambie on the Facebook website, the third Thursday in November 2015. "*That is* a culture of hatred, ignorance and white Australia, a culture that is repugnant."

A few weeks later, on the second Friday in December, James applauded Rahila Haidary, a Muslim Afghan. "*Wonderful to this lady stand up against thugs,*" he wrote, thugs being his compatriots defending their culture. "*Fantastic she is proud of her faith and culture. What an inspiration.*"

Another day later, James condemned Australians at Cronulla convening a halal-free barbecue for being proud of their culture. "*Nationalism, patriotism, racism. Seen the same to me. The ugly side of Australia.*"

Bogan is an Australian pejorative for working-class white people. "*Yep,*" wrote James, the second Saturday in March 2017, "*ban the bogans not the burka.*"

Wealthy white people don't like poor white people; our ideologies of inclusion are for other races, not ours. We've proceeded from neglect for our races and cultures to hostility towards them, we defenders of other races and cultures from ours.

Aficionados we may be for the arts, but when we own our culture, we don't share ownership with our race. Ours is the haute couture, European high culture: the hidden-away paintings, films, and books few people see, watch, or read.

The closest thing I've seen to a European art-house film reaching cinemas anywhere, let alone abroad, was *Russian Dolls* in 2005; my half-Lebanese friend Mark invited me to a screening in Centennial Park because his wife was otherwise engaged. The actresses had fine, lovely legs, but I lost count of how many times one walked in slowly swaying motion along a pretty, near-empty city street. Friends of different races lolled around their comfortably clean, crimeless lives, without a story to tell.

We pay attention to critical opinions, if we know what they are. In matters of leisure, we like what the experts like (even if we quietly, guiltily watch what they don't).

Artists are our favourite class, especially when they're coloured. *Granta* magazine listed Chinese-born Xiaolu Guo, resident in Hackney, as one of the twenty most promising British writers in 2013. She seems not to have seen herself as British. Her first novel, published the following year, was *I am China*.

We bestow upon them our awards and patronage, depending more on politics than merit. No stories we like more than refugees overcoming the adversities they tell us they've suffered, before finding happiness because we've admitted them to the West.

Vietnamese-born Anh Do received 2011 Australian Book Industry Awards for newcomer, biography, and book of the year for his memoir *The Happiest Refugee*, notwithstanding that journalist Michael Visontay ghost-wrote it. *"To my friend Michael Visontay,"* mentioned Do's acknowledgment, his only admission of a ghostwriter, *"who taught me how to write a book and helped me with structure and form."* Do claimed later that he revised the manuscript presented to him. Visontay received royalties.

Do's book sold well, as it would, but the fewer people who like what we like, the more elite we feel. Anything most people see, watch, and read disappears into being commercial, thereby universal.

Small audiences take great pride that the masses don't share their tastes with them, certain the masses can't understand what they understand. They're right.

Our haute couture makers demand to craft whatever they want, without interest in sales. No worker is more embroiled in production and no consumer more self-absorbed than is the artist consuming his art that no one else does. Her self-indulgent wallowing transfixes others who self-indulgently wallow, whatever anyone else thinks.

Our greatest arts came from artists inspired by something greater than themselves, like God or their race, country, or family. Having become individuals, we lack such inspiration.

The Blake Prize for religious art originally reflected Christianity being firmly enmeshed with art, as other religions weren't. Pursuing our multicultural vision, the prize came to reward art not revelling in religion but rejecting it. Rodney Pople's entry in the 2010 competition was concerned with paedophilia in the Roman Catholic Church. Fiona White won the human justice prize of five thousand dollars for a piece about racism.

Religious art became like other art. "I hope they feel something of life, an affirmation of being, which is a primary spiritual sensibility," said Leonard Brown, whose *If You Put Your Ear Close, You'll Hear it Breathing* won first prize and twenty thousand dollars. "With theology, as with art, there's no retirement." Yet, there was no theology in his art, nor was there art. That Brown had been ordained in the Russian Orthodox Church wasn't obvious.

If we're not corrupting our culture, we're advocating others. If we want inspiration, we look to other races.

In September 2012, while Muslims were chanting "Death to France" because a French magazine had published a cartoon depicting Mohammed, the Louvre Museum opened a wing of Islamic art so that French people would think better of Muslims. I dare say there were no images of paedophilia.

The most European of art forms include ballet, but ballet teachers and schools are a world unto themselves, with no sense of a society outside or of proportion inside. Any student not willing to disfigure every bone in her body isn't sufficiently dedicated. I've not seen any ballet since my daughters stopped learning.

I prefer opera. Richard H was group company secretary and general counsel of Australian National Line, before setting off to Europe to sing opera. He later returned to the law.

Around about the year 2000, the Australian Opera commissioned a study seeking reasons for the low ticket sales to seasons of opera at the Sydney Opera House, in spite of tens of thousands of people attending operas performed annually on the lawns of the Sydney Domain. Regular Opera House attendees believed most of the population didn't understand opera. With such an attitude, it was hardly surprising that most people declining to see opera in the Opera House did so because they didn't like the people who did.

We reserve the best of our cultural tradition to our miniature selves. When we want to expand the boundaries of our haute couture, we don't pursue the rest of our race: those fools who don't understand. We pursue everyone else.

"We...will do our utmost...to see in our audiences," said Lyndon Terracini, artistic director of Opera Australia, in 2011, "on our stages and in our orchestra pits, the faces of new and contemporary Australians, the faces of Aboriginal Australians, as well as our long-term traditional supporters. At Opera Australia we are committed to ensuring that great art embraces the faces which represent Australia in the twenty-first century."

Other races like seeing their race on the stage. We like seeing them, too. "I noticed recently in our extremely successful production of *La Boheme*," continued Terracini, "which has played to forty-five thousand people in Melbourne and Sydney, that when we had an African American soprano and a Korean tenor singing the leading roles, we had more audience members from those ethnic communities than we usually see in the theatre."

Chinese and Japanese operas, like other Asian, Arab, Jewish, and African arts and cultures, develop or don't according to their terms. They're in the hands of their races and countries. Our arts and cultures aren't in ours. "It will not work if our expectations continue to be for Asian artists to pretend to perform like Europeans," said Terracini, "while at the same time try to communicate with their ethnic audience."

We've sullied our great arts to deny us our greatness. In 2006, Hans Neuenfels directed a performance of Wolfgang Amadeus Mozart's *Idomeneo* by the German Opera in Berlin, which ended with King Idomeneo spattered in blood and placing the severed heads of Poseidon, Jesus, Buddha, and Mohammed on chairs. We didn't care, but the German Opera cancelled performances for fear of offending Muslims.

We don't emulate. We destroy.

There's no fusion in culture. People asserting their culture might allow theirs to be influenced. People not asserting their cultures let theirs be subsumed or abate.

Oratorios are large concert pieces involving music, choirs, and soloists, without the theatre of operas. The last Sunday in April 2012, I sat with three of my children before a performance of German composer George Frideric Handel's 1741 oratorio *Messiah* in what had been the Wesleyan church in Tryon Road, Lindfield. On a wall was the only war honour board I've seen speak of home, listing the names of those who'd fought and died "*For God, Home & Empire*," but the home and empire were no longer ours. When the Uniting church wasn't a venue for music, it was home to a Korean congregation. If an Australian congregation remained at the church, it was the old people serving tea and supper afterwards. No Korean attended the concert.

The most dedicated opera and symphony buff I know, my friend James expected immigrants to keep our British crown intact. In 2013, he saw some Asians playing bagpipes in school bands and thought that meant the country becoming Asian won't lose the last of our European character. (There were no suggestions of other races appropriating our culture by experiencing it.) "You're kidding yourself," I told him.

The only thing worse than the contempt that kills so much of our cultures, is the conceit that imagines other races maintaining the morsels we like. All it takes is a single Asian virtuoso to play a piece from old Europe for us to presume our cultures endure, but cultural archaeology is archaeology nevertheless. Our fine arts fade, before becoming something else. We can't expect other races to maintain our cultural heritage when we don't. If we don't rediscover our heritage and reclaim it for us, nobody else will sustain it.

The best we can hope is that mongrel arts remain with a little of our gene pools within them: some small influence our cultures have upon those cultures replacing them. Most likely, they won't.

Our cultural elite save only the culture we like. So much the individuals, we save it for ourselves. We're not trying to defend and develop our cultures, as other races do. We're just keeping corners in place for a time: the time we're alive to enjoy them, or at least appear to enjoy them. We love our high culture without loving our people, unconcerned that cultures can't exist without people to practice them. Without our peoples to possess them, our cultures can't survive us. What comes of our arts when we die doesn't matter to us, because we'll die knowing we appreciated them.

If we were as fair minded as we insist we are, we'd appreciate European races can do most things very well. We'd judge ourselves not by our most terrible years of twentieth-century war, but the totality of all we've done and tried valiantly to do. Thousands of years of history before 1914, and many a moment since then, testify to how great a people and peoples Europeans can be, in Europe and elsewhere. Cry, "God for Harry, England, and St George!"

I'm glad for the year I spent learning French and four years I spent learning German at school, as I'm glad for the few words of Czech (*zmrzlina*), Bulgarian (*Dobŭr den* and *Dobŭr nosht*), and other languages I picked up in my travels, sloppy as I might be speaking them. I can no longer be bothered expending my precious, short life on earth learning foreign words. English accords me a lifetime of great story, song, poetry, theatre, and oratory. With no need of any other tongue, I'd rather learn more of my language than others.

Other European languages do the same for their speakers, if what I've read of English-language translations do their literature and theatre justice. If any language but English is worth learning, it's Latin for what it means for my language, however antiquarian is the little Latin literature and theatre surviving.

Only peoples have cultural heritages and other cultures. Individuals have only their personal beliefs, lifestyles, and crafts.

To find exaltation, we need to be more than small individuals. We need to be peoples: reclaiming and reviving our cultures, to develop as we decide. We have no one with whom to share our personal glory if we don't participate in our people's glory and let our people participate in what is personally ours. A symphony isn't a symphony without someone to play it and someone to hear.

BIBLIOGRAPHY, REFERENCES

Articles

Ahmed, Tanveer, 'Our opportunity in Pakistan,' *The Sydney Morning Herald* newspaper, 13 May 2009.

Antonova, Maria, 'Russia's new culture policy a weapon against West,' *Agence France-Presse* news service published at *Yahoo! News*, 18 April 2014.

Auerbach, Taylor, 'Interesting Korea choice! Blonde Brazilian man obsessed with South Korea undergoes 10 rounds of surgery to look 'more Asian',' *Daily Mail* newspaper, 2 June 2014.

Bastow, Clem, 'Cultural theft,' *Daily Life* in *The Sydney Morning Herald* newspaper, 2 March 2012. Uncredited, 'Victoria's Secret 'racist' outfit sparks outrage,' *News Limited Network*, 25 September 2012.

Bernstein, Richard, 'Hometown Snubs Schwarzenegger Over Death Penalty,' *The New York Times* newspaper, 27 December 2005.

Bibby, Paul, 'End of an era as developers move in to Spanish quarter,' *The Sydney Morning Herald* newspaper, 18 April 2009.

Blade, 'Paris holds first 'Black Fashion Week',' *France 24* news, 6 October 2012.

Bodkin, Peter, 'Choirgirl, 15, on murder charge,' *The Daily Telegraph* newspaper, 22 March 2013. Clementine Cuneo, 'Patrick Crowe stabbed to death during night out with friends in Parramatta,' *The Daily Telegraph* newspaper, 9 July 2012.

Bolt, Andrew, 'Emphasis on tribes is a bad move,' *Herald Sun* newspaper, 26 February 2011.

Borden, Sam, 'Kiwanuka Goes Home, but His Heart Is Far Away,' *The New York Times* newspaper, 29 January 2012.

Byrnes, Holly and Henry Budd, 'True blue Oprah keeps it real with backyard barbecue and VB,' *The Daily Telegraph* newspaper, 13 December 2010.

Carson, Vanda, 'Historic Point Piper home set for the wrecking ball,' *The Sydney Morning Herald* newspaper, 29 December 2010.

Carty, Lisa, 'Open and shut case as rat-infested bakery fined $45,000,' *The Sydney Morning Herald* newspaper, 6 September 2009.

Edwards, Tito, 'Sharia Law and the U.S. Constitution,' *American*

Catholic magazine, 25 June 2010.

Farrelly, Elizabeth, 'Let's shoot straight on gay marriage,' *The Sydney Morning Herald* newspaper, 25 August 2011.

FitzSimons, Peter, 'I'm a non-believer, loud and proud,' *The Sun Herald* newspaper, 19 September 2010. Tim Blair, 'Stupidity of lefty riot apologists,' *The Daily Telegraph* newspaper, 15 August 2011. Peter FitzSimons, 'And I was just getting started – Church and hate,' *The Sydney Morning Herald* newspaper, 18 December 2011.

Flegenheimer, Matt, "Carlin Street' Resisted By His Old Church. Was It Something He Said?' *The New York Times* newspaper, 25 October 2011.

Goddard, Jacqui, 'Britney Spears 'worth $120m to US economy',' *The Telegraph* newspaper, 2 February 2008.

Gorman, Alyx, 'The 10 Worst Trends of 2011,' *The Vine* at *The Sydney Morning Herald* newspaper, 29 December 2011.

Hale, Virginia, 'Top Academic: Muslims Would Not Tolerate Multiculturalism in Islamic Countries,' *Breitbart News*, 2 September 2016.

Hamilton, Jane, 'This little piggy was banned for religious reasons,' *The Sun* newspaper, 16 November 2010.

Hayward, Andrea, 'Govt presents new multiculturalism policy,' *The Sydney Morning Herald* newspaper, 16 February 2011. Chris Bowen, 'What makes multiculturalism great is mutual respect,' published on 17 February 2011.

Herman, Judi, 'Visiting Mr Mitchell: Warren Mitchell talks to Judi Herman about 'Visiting Mr Green',' *All About Jewish Theatre*, 2008.

Heslam, Jessica, 'Fun takes a holiday in Somerville,' *The Boston Herald* newspaper, 14 October 2011.

Hohmann, Leo, 'Germany promotes non-Muslim women wearing hijab,' *World Net Daily*, 15 September 2016.

Jinman, Richard and Kylie Davis, 'Police warn Biennale over chicken video,' *The Sydney Morning Herald* newspaper, 18 June 2008.

Lentini, Rosemarie, 'Is our 'Austrayan' twang on way out?' *The Daily Telegraph* newspaper, 26 January 2010. Uncredited, 'FYI: China wants TV English ban,' *Agence France-Presse* news service published in *The Sydney Morning Herald* newspaper, 7 April 2010.

Masanauskas, John, 'Hefty bill for Muslim women's privacy at public swimming pool,' *Herald Sun* newspaper, 11 February 2011.

Matthews, Lee, 'Artist drags 25kg block of ice through city,' *Manawatu Standard* newspaper, 5 May 2012.

McDonald, John, 'Award has become an unholy irrelevance,' commenting on "An enormous spiritual presence' wins Blake Prize for artist,' *The Sydney Morning Herald* newspaper, 3 September 2010.

McLaughlin, Eliott, and Deanna Hackney, 'Democrats want John Wayne Airport renamed after 'I believe in white supremacy' interview resurfaces,' *Cable News Network*, 29 June 2020.

Mezzofiore, Gianluca, 'Ramadan 2014: We Can Deport Anyone Who Eats, Drinks or Smokes, Saudi Arabia Tells Non-Muslims,' *International Business Times*, 26 June 2014. Uncredited, 'Saudi Arabia's Sharia Court Introduces 10 Years Jail Term for Anyone Who Celebrates Christmas,' *J & K News Service*, 25 December 2015.

Munro, Kelsey, 'A Parisian touch for Penrith future,' *The Sydney Morning Herald* newspaper, 26 October 2011.

Nicholls, Sean and Matt Wade, 'Sydney should embrace Asia, says O'Farrell,' *The Sydney Morning Herald* newspaper, 7 November 2011. Andrew West, 'Vibrant suburbs offer more comfort for new migrants,' *The Sydney Morning Herald* newspaper, 8 November 2011.

O'Brien, Natalie, 'Liverpool Council upsets Orthodox community by leaving pork off the menu for interfaith lunch,' *The Sydney Morning Herald* newspaper, 26 July 2015.

Paton, Graeme, 'Asian sex gang 'cultural norms',' *The Telegraph* newspaper, 10 May 2012.

Penberthy, David, 'A cringeworthy spectacle from a country we outgrew,' *The Punch* website, 10 June 2012, quoting Theodore Dalrymple in the *Spectator* magazine.

Poulter, Sean, 'Subway removes ham and bacon from nearly 200 stores and offers halal meat only after 'strong demand' from Muslims,' *Daily Mail* newspaper, 30 April 2014.

Robinson, Georgina, 'Milli O'Nair's happy life cut horribly short in freak accident,' *The Sydney Morning Herald* newspaper, 12 May 2009. Uncredited, 'Friends say farewell as Milli takes wing,' *The Byron Shire Echo* newspaper, 19 May 2009. Saffron Howden, 'Man charged over cyclist's death,' *The Northern Star* newspaper,

2 June 2009.

Rosenberg, Michael, 'Tiger Woods rules controversy showed a little common sense won't kill the game,' *Sports Illustrated* magazine, 13 April 2013.

Serpe, Gina, 'Nicki Minaj 'Vulgar' Grammys Exorcism Angers Catholic League,' *Entertainment (E!) On-line*, 13 February 2012.

Smith, Alexandra, 'Fiesta fiasco: Sydney University cancels Mexican party theme,' *The Sydney Morning Herald* newspaper, 13 November 2014.

Totaro, Paola, 'Elders tell museums: send our people home,' *The Sydney Morning Herald* newspaper, 13 May 2009.

Uncredited, 'Aboriginal leader lashes at assimilation,' *Australian Associated Press* news service published in *The Sydney Morning Herald* newspaper, 8 August 2009.

Uncredited, 'Alec Baldwin forced to apologise to the Philippines over 'mail-order bride' jibe,' *Agence France-Presse* news service published in *The Sydney Morning Herald* newspaper, 22 May 2009.

Uncredited, 'Australia to host Regional Pravasi Bharatiya Divas 2013,' *The Indian Express* newspaper, 30 May 2013.

Uncredited, 'Cleaner throws out 'rubbish' Sala Murat artwork,' *BBC News*, 20 February 2014.

Uncredited, 'Couple kept sham marriage to stop violent reprisals,' *The Sydney Morning Herald* newspaper, 31 July 2010.

Uncredited, 'Crucifixes in classrooms 'violate rights',' *Agence France-Presse* news service, 4 November 2009. Paul Sims, 'Compulsory crucifixes in Italian classrooms? Not a good sign,' *The Guardian* newspaper, 25 March 2011.

Uncredited, 'Dad in pork issue claims he is not Muslim,' *The Malaysia Star* newspaper, 12 November 2010. Staff writers, 'Boy caned for bringing pork to school,' *News Core*, 13 November 2010.

Uncredited, 'Empty Room Wins $55,000 Art Prize,' *The Sydney Morning Herald* newspaper, 10 December 2001. Uncredited, 'Empty Room Wins Turner Art Prize,' at *Cable News Network*, 10 December 2001.

Uncredited, 'Ex-Gaddafi colonel says regime crumbling,' *Agence France-Presse* news service published in *The Sydney Morning Herald* newspaper, 14 August 2011.

Uncredited, 'Full-size Forbidden City gates replica planned for NSW theme park,' *The Sydney Morning Herald* newspaper, 4

December 2012.

Uncredited, 'Islamic group banned from UCL following gender segregation row,' *National Secular Society*, 12 March 2013.

Uncredited, 'Liberals committed to 'cultural diversity',' *Australian Associated Press* news service published at *Yahoo! News*, 24 February 2011.

Uncredited, 'Mandatory Arabic Classes Coming to Mansfield,' *CBS Dallas Fort Worth*, 7 February 2011. Uncredited, 'Mansfield Arabic Program on Hold,' *CBS Dallas Fort Worth*, 8 February 2011.

Uncredited, 'NASA Chief: Next Frontier Better Relations With Muslim World,' *Fox News*, 5 July 2010.

Uncredited, 'Now It's a Negro Drive for Segregation,' *U.S. News & World Report*, 30 March 1964, republished by *U.S. News*, 16 May 2008.

Uncredited, 'Relax, says McGuire on 'land of falafel' fallout,' *Australian Associated Press* news service published in *The Sydney Morning Herald* newspaper, 11 February 2011.

Uncredited, 'Somalia and Brunei ban Christmas celebrations,' *Agence France-Presse* news service published at *Al Jazeera* news, 23 December 2015.

Uncredited, 'Toronto's glass condos face short lifespan, experts say,' *CBC News Toronto* published at *Yahoo! News*, 15 November 2011.

Williams, Matt, 'Tilda Swinton sleeps in glass box for art installation at MoMA,' *The Guardian* newspaper, 24 March 2013.

Williamson, Marcus, 'Tom Sharpe: Comic novelist and satirist who created the Wilt series and Porterhouse Blue,' *Independent* newspaper, 7 June 2013.

Yates, Lyn, 'New curriculum will ultimately mould our national identity,' *The Sydney Morning Herald* newspaper, 6 April 2011. Steve Lewis, 'Coalition fury at Labor school lessons,' *The Daily Telegraph* newspaper, 4 June 2010.

Young, Ian writing as the Hongcouver, 'Born in China, Joy Mo blames rich mainlanders for Vancouver's housing woes,' *South China Morning Post* newspaper, 4 December 2013.

Books

Brown, Dan, born 1964, *Angels And Demons* (2000).

Brown, Dan, born 1964, *The Da Vinci Code* (2003).
Camus, Albert, 1913-1960, *L'Étranger* (*The Stranger* or *The Outsider*, 1942).
Chaucer, Geoffrey, circa 1343-1400, *The Canterbury Tales* (1475).
Dawkins, Richard, born 1941, *The God Delusion* (2006). Fiona Macrae, 'Atheist Richard Dawkins blames Muslims for 'importing creationism' into classrooms,' *Daily Mail* newspaper, 5 August 2008. Editor's Note to the letter 'Gnostic Christians,' *Creation* magazine, March to May 2009.
Descartes, René, 1596-1650, *Discourse on the Method* (1637) and *Meditations on First Philosophy* (1641), published together as *Discourse on Method and Meditations* (1998). The Latin phrase *Cogito ergo sum* appeared in *Principles of Philosophy* (1644).
Do, Anh, *The Happiest Refugee* (2010). Henrietta Cook, 'Anh Do had help on prize-winning book,' *The Age* newspaper, 27 July 2015.
Dunstan, Keith, 1925-2013, *Ratbags* (1979) described Arthur Stace.
Gibbs, George and Oliver Wolcott, *Memoirs of the Administrations of Washington and John Adams: edited from the papers of Oliver Wolcott, Secretary of the Treasury* (1846).
Guo, Xiaolu, born 1973, *I am China* (2014).
Hawking, Stephen, born 1942, *A Brief History of Time* (1988).
Hitler, Adolf, 1889-1945, and Martin Bormann, 1900-1945, *Hitler's Table Talk* (1951).
Hitler, Adolf, 1889-1945, *Mein Kampf* (1925).
Keith, Agnes Newton, 1901-1982, *Three Came Home* (1948).
Menzies, Gavin, born 1937, *1421: The Year China Discovered the World* (2002). *Four Corners* television (1961 onwards), 'Junk History' (reporter Quentin McDermott, broadcast 31 July 2006).
Menzies, Gavin, born 1937, *1434: The Year a Magnificent Chinese Fleet Sailed to Italy and Ignited the Renaissance* (2008).
Nietzsche, Friedrich Wilhelm, 1844-1900, *Also Sprach Zarathustra* (*Thus Spoke Zarathustra*, 1883).
Orwell, George, born Eric Blair, 1903-1950, *1984* known also as *Nineteen Eighty-Four* (1949).
Plimer, Ian, *Telling Lies for God: Reason vs Creationism* (1994).
Pliny the Elder, born Gaius Plinius Secundus, 23-79, *Naturalis Historia* (*Natural History*, ten volumes).
Pratten, Chris, *Summer Hill* (1999), Ashfield & District Historical Society.

Richards, Frank, *Old Soldiers Never Die* (1933). Peter Simkins and Paul Fussell were interviewed in the television documentary *The Great War and the Shaping Of the 20th Century* (1996).
Richardson, Henry Handel (born Ethel Florence Lindesay Richardson), 1870-1946, *The Fortunes of Richard Mahony* (1930). Michael Heyward, 'Literary heroes forgotten,' *The Sydney Morning Herald* newspaper, 21 January 2012.
Roebuck, Peter Michael, 1956-2011, *Sometimes I Forgot to Laugh* (2004).
Rogers, Joel Augustus, 1880 or 1883-1966, *Sex and Race: Negro-Caucasian Mixing in all Ages and all Lands* (three volumes). He published all his works at his own expense.
Sales, William, *From Civil Rights to Black Liberation* (1994). Page 87 referred to Malcolm X.
Salinger, J D, 1919-2012, *The Catcher in the Rye* (1951).
Thoreau, Henry David, 1817-1862, *Walden* (1854).
Toland, John, *Adolf Hitler: The Definitive Biography* (1992). Page 507 referred to Hitler's Roman Catholicism.
Uncredited, *Daring Book for Girls*. Judy Skatssoon, 'Uproar over girls playing didgeridoo,' *Australian Associated Press* news service, 2 September 2008.
Williams, Roy, born 1962, *God, Actually* (2010).
Williams, Roy, born 1962, *Post-God Nation* (2015).

Carols and Hymns

'Abide with Me.'
'Amazing Grace.'
'Away in a Manger.'
'God Save the Queen.'
'Hark the Herald Angels Sing.'
'How Great Thou Art.'
'I vow to thee, my country.'
'Jerusalem.'
'Onward Christian Soldiers.'
'When I Survey the Wondrous Cross.'

Comics

Horswill, Ian, 'A half black half Latino Spider Man is followed by

DC Comics' Green Lantern Arab Muslim superhero,' *Reuters* news service published at *News Limited Network*, 7 September 2012.

Uncredited, 'Marvel Comics debuts female Muslim superhero,' *The Telegraph* newspaper, 5 November 2013.

Essays

Orwell, George, 'Why I Write' (1946).

Films

1917 (2019)

3 Acts of Murder (2009), written by Ian David.

Abyss, The (1989), written and directed by James Cameron.

Accused, The, (1988). Paul Edward Parker, 'Juries hear Big Dan's rape case,' *The Providence Journal* newspaper, 1 November 1999.

Alice in Wonderland (2010). Lewis Carroll, born Charles Dodgson, 1832-1898, wrote *Alice's Adventures in Wonderland* (1865) and *Through The Looking-Glass* (1871).

Annie (1982) and *Annie* (2014), based upon a 1977 musical. Harold Gray, 1894-1968, created the comic series *Little Orphan Annie*. Quinn Costello, 'Target's Ads for New 'Annie'-Inspired Collection Draw Controversy,' *Hollywood Reporter*, 30 December 2014.

Batman Begins (2005), based upon the D.C. Comics series.

Belle (2013), written by Nigerian-born Misan Sagay.

Blade Runner (1982). Philip Dick, 1928-1982, wrote *Do Androids Dream of Electric Sheep?* (1968).

Captain America: The First Avenger (2011), based on the Marvel Comics character created by Joseph Henry Simon (born Hymie Simon), 1913-2011, and Jack Kirby (born Jacob Kurtzberg), 1917-1994. Anneta Konstantinides, 'New Captain America comic sees superhero Sam Wilson take on and defeat anti-immigration vigilantes,' *Daily Mail* newspaper, 19 October 2015.

Cinderella (2015). Charles Perrault, 1628-1703, *Histoires ou contes du temps passé* (*Stories or Fairy Tales from Past Times with Morals*, 1697). Kenneth Branagh directed. Nonso Anozie played the captain.

Darkest Hour (2017)

Day the Earth Stood Still, The (1951), written by Edward North,

1911-1990. Harry Bates, 1900-1981, wrote the short story *Farewell to the Master* (1940).

Doctor Dolittle (1967) and (1998), inspired by the writings of Hugh Lofting, 1886-1947, starring Rex Harrison and Eddie Murphy respectively.

Dr. No (1962), based upon the 1958 novel by Ian Fleming, 1908-1964.

E.T. The Extra Terrestrial (1982), written by Melissa Mathison, 1950-2015.

Emma (1996), based upon the 1815 novel by Jane Austen, 1775-1817.

Flash Gordon (1980), based upon the comic series created by Alex Raymond, 1909-1956.

Gran Torino (2008), written by Nick Schenk, born 1965.

Grand Budapest Hotel, The (2014), written and directed by Wes Anderson, born 1969.

Hunted (1952), written by Jack Whittingham, 1910-1972. Dirk Bogarde played Chris Lloyd. Ghana-born Harry Quashie played the Coloured Man.

Hurricane, The (1999), adapted from Rubin "Hurricane" Carter, born 1937, *The 16th Round* (1974) and Sam Chaiton and Terry Swinton, *Lazarus and the Hurricane* (1991). Milan Simonich, 'Rubin 'Hurricane' Carter: Film of his life a contender,' *Pittsburgh Post-Gazette* newspaper, 27 March 2000. Lona Manning, 'The Hurricane Hoax,' *Crime Magazine*.

I am Legend (2007) starring Will Smith, inspired by Richard Matheson's novel *I am Legend* (1954), as was *The Last Man on Earth* (1964) and *The Omega Man* (1971).

Into the Woods (2014), based upon the 1986 musical with lyrics by Stephen Sondheim, born 1930, and book by James Lapine, born 1949, inspired by *Grimms' Fairy Tales* by Jacob Grimm, 1785-1863, and Wilhelm Grimm, 1786-1859.

Jungle Book, The (2016), inspired by the 1894 book by Rudyard Kipling, 1865-1936.

Little Big Man (1970), based upon the 1964 comic novel by Thomas Berger.

Live and Let Die (1973), based upon the 1954 novel by Ian Fleming, 1908-1964.

Lost World, The (2001). Sir Arthur Conan Doyle, 1859-1930, wrote the 1912 novel.

Paddington (2014), inspired by the books by Michael Bond, born 1926.

Pawnbroker, The (1965), based upon the 1961 novel by Jewish writer Edward Wallant, 1926-1962. Mystery Man, 'Sex in Screenwriting,' published at *The Story Department* website, 19 July 2010.

Peyton Place (1957).

Prince of Persia: The Sands of Time (2010), based upon the video game created by Jordan Mechner, born 1964. Sara Haghdoosti, 'Jake Gyllenhaal stole my identity and my video game,' *The Punch* website, 7 June 2010.

Quantum of Solace (2008), based upon the James Bond character created by Ian Fleming, 1908-1964. James Lachno and PA, 'Pierce Brosnan backs first black James Bond,' *The Telegraph* newspaper, 13 April 2013.

Russian Dolls, or *Les Poupées russes* (2005), written and directed by Cédric Klapisch, born 1961.

Saving Private Ryan (1998), written by Robert Rodat, born 1953, and directed by Steven Spielberg, born 1946.

Skyfall (2012), based upon the James Bond character created by Ian Fleming, 1908-1964. Naomie Harris played Eve Moneypenny.

Snow White and the Seven Dwarfs (1937), based upon a German fairy tale published in the 1812 collection of *Grimms' Fairy Tales* by Jacob Grimm, 1785-1863, and Wilhelm Grimm, 1786-1859.

Star Wars I: The Phantom Menace (1999), written and directed by George Lucas, born 1944. Jar Jar Jinks was primarily computer generated, with the voice of black American, Ahmed Best. The character also appeared in the next two Star Wars films *The Attack of the Clones* (2002) and *Revenge of the Sith* (2005).

Starman (1984), written by Bruce Evans and Raynold Gideon.

Stickup, The (2001), written and directed by Rowdy Herrington.

Thor (2011), based upon a series of Marvel Comics.

Total Recall (1990), written by Ronald Shusett, Dan O'Bannon, and Gary Goldman. Arnold Schwarzenegger played Douglas Quaid.

Way, The (2010), starring Martin Sheen and written and directed by his son Emilio Estevez. Estevez talked about the film on *The Busted Halo Show with Father Dave* on radio station Sirius XM in Los Angeles, California on 6 April 2010.

What's Cooking? (2001), written by Gurinder Chadha and Paul Mayeda Berges. Peter Thompson reviewed it on *Sunday* (1981

onwards), Nine Network, Australia, broadcast on 13 May 2001.
When Harry Met Sally... (1989), written by Nora Ephron.

Judgments

Church of the Holy Trinity v United States, 143 U.S. 457 (1892).
United States v Macintosh, 283 U.S. 605 (1931).
Updegraph v Commonwealth, 11 Serg. & Rawle 394 (Pa. 1824).

Operas

Idomeneo (1780), written by Wolfgang Amadeus Mozart, 1756-1791.
La Boheme (1896), written by Giacomo Puccini, 1858-1924. Lyndon Terracini, 'Opera must reflect modern Australia, or become irrelevant,' *The Sydney Morning Herald* newspaper, 3 November 2011.
Madame Butterfly (1904), written by Giacomo Puccini, 1858-1924.

Oratorios

Messiah (1741), written by George Frideric Handel, born Georg Friedrich Händel, 1685-1759.

Parliamentary Reports

Hogg, Quintin McGarel, *Hansard*, Commons Sitting, Orders of the Day, 27 February 1968. Christian Joppke, born 1959, *Immigration and the Nation-State: The United States, Germany and Great Britain* (1999), Oxford University Press, page 110.

Plays

Entertainer, The (1957), written by John Osborne, 1929-1994. Laurence Olivier played Archie Rice in the 1960 film.
Glass Menagerie, The (1944), written by Tennessee Williams, 1911-1983.
Henry V (1599, probably), written by William Shakespeare, baptised 1564-1616. At Act 3, Scene 1, King Henry V says, "Cry 'God for Harry, England, and Saint George!'"
Macbeth (1606, probably), written by William Shakespeare, baptised

1564-1616.

Richard III (1592, probably), written by William Shakespeare, baptised 1564-1616.

Romeo and Juliet (1591-1595, probably), written by William Shakespeare, baptised 1564-1616.

Woman of No Importance, A (1893), written by Oscar Wilde, 1854-1900.

Poems

Charge of the Light Brigade, The (1854), written by Alfred, Lord Tennyson, 1809-1892.

Odyssey (8th or 7th century B.C.), accredited to Homer, dates of birth and death unknown.

Paradise Lost (1667), written by John Milton, 1608-1674.

Peace (1914), written by Rupert Brooke, 1887-1915. Gina McColl, 'Fighting words: Do Australian jihadis have anything in common with World War I Anzacs?' *The Sydney Morning Herald* newspaper, 25 April 2015.

Wreck of the Hesperus, The (1842), written by Henry Wadsworth Longfellow, 1807-1882.

Songs

'FranSSe,' sung by Mounsier R. Tim Hodson, 'A Very Brief Critique of Radio Quotas Part 1,' *Perfect Sound Forever* magazine, May 2006.

'MacArthur Park' (1968), by Jimmy Webb, born 1946, first recorded in 1968 by Richard Harris, 1930-2002. MacArthur Park is a park in Los Angeles.

'Magical Mystery Tour' (1967), by the Beatles, which was the subject of an album and a short film *Magical Mystery Tour* that year.

'Philosopher's Drinking Song' (1973), known also as 'Bruce's Philosophers Song' or 'Bruce's Song,' written by Eric Idle, born 1943, for the album *Free Record Given Away with the Monty Python Matching Tie and Handkerchief*, released in 1973.

'Scarborough Fair,' an old Yorkshire ballad, drawn upon by Paul Simon for his and Art Garfunkel's 1966 album *Parsley, Sage, Rosemary, and Thyme*.

'There'll Always Be an England' (1939), composed and written by Albert Rostron Parker, 1914-1974, and Charles Hugh Owen Ferry, 1907-1995. The song closed the British version of Deanna Durbin's 1941 film *Nice Girl?*

'Unconditionally' (2013). Hardeep Phull, 'Katy Perry's 'offensive' appearance at AMAs,' *New York Post* newspaper, 25 November 2013.

'White Christmas' (1940), written by Irving Berlin, born Israel Isidore Beilin, 1888-1989, and sung most famously by Bing Crosby, 1903-1977.

'With God on Our Side' (1963), by Bob Dylan, appearing on the 1964 album *The Times They Are A-Changin'*.

Symphonies

Symphony Number 6 in F major, Opus 68, known also as *The Pastoral Symphony*, (1808), composed by Ludwig van Beethoven, 1770-1827.

Television Programmes

7.30 Report, The (1986 onwards), 'Hindmarsh bridge controversy continues' (reporter Anne Barker, broadcast 21 August 2001), Australian Broadcasting Corporation.

Addams Family, The (1964-1966), based upon characters created in 1938 by cartoonist Charles Addams, 1912-1988.

Alf (1986-1990).

Alleyn Mysteries, The: Death at the Bar (1992), inspired by the 1940 novel by Ngaio Marsh, 1895-1982.

Arthur (1996 onwards).

Bachelor, The and *The Bachelorette* (2002 onwards and 2003 onwards). Sheila Burke, 'Lawsuit claims 'Bachelor' show discriminates,' *Associated Press* news service, 18 April 2012. Matt Young, 'Is the Bachelor racially insensitive? Channel 10 responds to criticism,' *News Limited Network,* 1 August, 2014.

Bewitched (1964-1972).

Brum (1992 onwards).

Casanova (2005), written by Russell Davies, inspired by Giacomo Casanova, 1725-1798, *Histoire de ma vie (Story of My Life)*.

Crusoe (2008-2009), especially the fourth episode 'High Water,'

inspired by Daniel Defoe, circa 1660-1731, *Robinson Crusoe* (1719).
Doctor Who (1963-1989, 2005 onward).
Doctor Who: The Ark in Space (1975).
Doctor Who: The End of the World (2005), written by Russell Davies.
Doctor Who: The Talons of Weng-Chiang (1977).
Downton Abbey (2010-2015). Patrick Foster, 'God banished from Downton Abbey, says show's historical advisor,' *The Telegraph* newspaper, 15 November 2015. *Southern Cross* magazine, December 2015.
Dynasty (1981-1989). Diahann Carroll was interviewed for *Theatreweek* magazine, 1 to 7 January 1996.
Elementary (2012 onwards). Lucy Liu played Doctor Watson.
Equaliser, The (1985-1989). Edward Woodward played Robert McCall. Denzel Washington played the role in the 2014 film.
Fugitive, The (1963-1967). Barry Morse played Philip Gerard.
Gruen Transfer, The (2008 onwards), Australian Broadcasting Corporation Television. The edition broadcast on 13 May 2009 omitted the Fat Pride advertisement and panel discussion. Arjun Ramachandran, 'How 'fat chick' furore made adman think,' *The Sydney Morning Herald* newspaper, 18 May 2009.
Love Thy Neighbour (1972-1977).
Marple (2004 onwards), inspired by the novels of Agatha Christie, 1890-1976.
Marple: By the Pricking of My Thumbs (2006), inspired by the 1968 novel by Agatha Christie, 1890-1976, with comments posted in the *Internet Movie Database* after its broadcast on Channel ABC1, Australia, on 26 December 2008.
Marple: Ordeal by Innocence (2007), inspired by the 1958 novel by Agatha Christie, 1890-1976.
Marple: The Moving Finger (2006), inspired by the 1942 novel by Agatha Christie, 1890-1976.
Marple: The Sittaford Mystery (2006), inspired by the 1931 novel by Agatha Christie, 1890-1976, with comments posted on the *Internet Movie Database* after its broadcast on Channel ABC1, Australia, on 16 January 2009.
Marple: Why Didn't They Ask Evans? (2009), inspired by the 1934 novel by Agatha Christie, 1890-1976.
Monster Warriors (2006-2008), created by Wilson Coneybeare.
Mork & Mindy (1978-1982).

Munsters, The (1964-1966).

My Favourite Martian (1963-1966).

Poirot: Appointment with Death (2008), inspired by the 1938 novel by Agatha Christie, 1890-1976.

Police Squad! (1982). American Broadcasting Company entertainment president Tony Thomopoulos discussed it on an episode of the television series *Entertainment Tonight* (1981 onwards).

Ripping Yarns (1976-1979), especially the pilot episode 'Tomkinson's Schooldays' (1976).

Soap (1977-1981).

Star Trek (1966-1969), created by Gene Roddenberry.

Tudors, The (2007-2010).

V (1983, 1984-1985), created by Kenneth Johnson, inspired by the 1935 novel *It Can't Happen Here* by Sinclair Lewis, 1885-1951.

Victoria (2016-2018), especially the 2nd series (2017), created by Daisy Goodwin.

ABOUT THE AUTHOR

Simon Lennon has travelled throughout Europe, America, Australasia, Asia, and the South Pacific, seeing how similar European peoples are to each other (wherever we live) and how different we of the West are to everyone else. He has university bachelor's degrees in science and law and university master's degrees in commerce and business. He is married with six children.

His non-fiction collection *The West* comprises the following sixteen books:

Mending the West
The Unnatural West: An Overview
The Tribeless West: An Overview
The Homeless West: An Overview
The Vanishing West: An Overview

Individualism
Western Individualism
The End of Natural Selection
The Need for Nations

Identity
People's Identity: Race and Racism
Of Whom We're Born: Race and Family
Biological Us: Gender and Sexuality

Nationalism
A Land to Belong: Nationalism
The Failure of Multiculturalism

Cultures
Reclaiming Western Cultures
Christendom Lost
Aiding Islam

He is also the author of another non-fiction book, two collections of short stories, and five novels.

www.ingramcontent.com/pod-product-compliance
Lightning Source LLC
LaVergne TN
LVHW041622070426
835507LV00008B/402